THE CORONA LIBRARY

BRITISH HONDURAS

BRITISH HONDURAS

BY
A. R. GREGG

LONDON
HER MAJESTY'S STATIONERY OFFICE
1968

First published 1968

© *Crown copyright 1968*

Published by
HER MAJESTY'S STATIONERY OFFICE

To be purchased from
49 High Holborn, London w.c.1
423 Oxford Street, London w.1
13A Castle Street, Edinburgh 2
109 St. Mary Street, Cardiff CF1 1JW
Brazennose Street, Manchester 2
50 Fairfax Street, Bristol BS1 3DE
258–259 Broad Street, Birmingham 1
7–11 Linenhall Street, Belfast BT2 8AY
or through any bookseller

Price £1 0s. 0d. net

THE CORONA LIBRARY

A series of illustrated volumes dealing with the United Kingdom's dependent territories, the way their peoples live, and how they are governed. The books were produced initially under the sponsorship of the Colonial Office, which was merged in 1966 with the Commonwealth Relations Office to form the Commonwealth Office. The series has been designed to fill the place between official Blue Books on the one hand and the writings of occasional visitors on the other, to be authoritative and readable, and to give a vivid yet accurate picture. The books are written by authors whose qualifications include, where possible, experience of colonial administration and first-hand knowledge of the territory concerned. Neither Her Majesty's Government in the United Kingdom nor the governments of the territories necessarily associate themselves with the personal views expressed by the authors. Each volume contains maps and is fully illustrated.

FOREWORD
TO THE CORONA LIBRARY

By the Rt. Hon. Sir Winston S. Churchill

K.G., O.M., C.H., M.P.

Chartwell, September 1956

NOT since the days of the Roman Empire has a single nation carried so great a responsibility for the lives of men and woman born outside her shores as Great Britain does today. Within her forty or so dependent territories dwell eighty million people for whose welfare and enlightenment Britain is, to a greater or lesser degree, answerable.

There has been no lack of critics, at home and abroad, to belittle Britain's colonial achievement and to impugn her motives. But the record confounds them. Look where you will, you will find that the British have ended wars, put a stop to savage customs, opened churches, schools and hospitals, built railways, roads and harbours, and developed the natural resources of the countries so as to mitigate the almost universal, desperate poverty. They have given freely in money and materials and in the services of a devoted band of Civil Servants; yet no tax is imposed upon any of the colonial peoples that is not spent by their own governments on projects for their own good.

I write 'their own governments' advisedly, for however much diverse conditions may necessitate different approaches, the British have for long had one goal in view for their overseas territories: their ultimate development into nations freely associated within the Commonwealth framework. The present state of the Commonwealth is the proof of the sincerity of this policy.

It is because I believe that Britain's colonial record is too little known and her policies too little understood that I welcome the books of the Corona Library. The aim of these books is to present a contemporary portrait, at once reliable and attractive, of each territory. I warmly commend the series to the attention of the public at home and abroad, for if these publications do even a little to clear away the clouds of misunderstandings and prejudice that have gathered round the very idea of colonial government, they will have been well worth while.

Winston S. Churchill

CONTENTS

PLATES

*Acknowledgments for photographs on plates I and II are due to
the British Information Department, British Honduras*

BOOK JACKET

designed by Janet Archer

Front: Artist's impression of Belize City from Belize River. Surrounded by mangrove swamps, the city is a strange mixture of old colonial structures, wooden frame buildings and new concrete buildings. In a long-term development programme, the new capital has been placed out of serious danger from hurricane winds and high water, some 50 miles away, near the Belize River and the village of Roaring Creek.

Back cover: The scores of cays and the barrier reef – the second largest in the world – are not the only assets of the off-shore waters. Beneath the sea lies a strange, beautiful world of coral and colourful fish; the crystal clear waters enable divers to take colour photographs from as far down as 60 to 80 feet.

ILLUSTRATIONS

by Denzie D. Belisle, British Honduras

FRONTISPIECE

Stepped pyramid at Altun Ha. Excavation continues at this Maya ceremonial centre, 30 miles from Belize City. Several valuable Maya finds have been unearthed during the work done here and elsewhere under the auspices of the British Honduras Department of Archaeology.

ENDPAPERS

A drawing of Belize from Fort St. George, 1842. The original colour print came from Government House, Belize City.

1. FIRST IMPRESSIONS

THE colony of British Honduras stretches 175 miles from north to south and about 75 from east to west. Turned on its side, the territory would fit snugly into the south of England, from London to Exeter and from the Thames to the Channel. It is situated between the 16th and 18th parallels of North Latitude, and between 88 and 90 degrees West. The area has been determined at 8,866 square miles. The population in 1967 was over 110,000.

On the north, the Hondo River separates the country from the Mexican state of Quintana Roo. To the south it is divided from Guatemala by the Sarstoon River. To the west are the Guatemalan departments of Izabal and Petén, with their sparse population of Indians, who change location from year to year and for whom the frontier does not exist; they drift according to ancient custom between British Honduras and Guatemala. On the east is the Caribbean Sea, the nearest land, the island of Jamaica, being 665 miles away.

To go to British Honduras once meant a trip to Jamaica, and the uncertainty of connections from Kingston – waiting for a boat. Nowadays most travellers fly, having a choice of several routes. Perhaps the most direct from Europe is by British Overseas Airways to Miami via Bermuda and the Bahamas, and there take one of the Central American airlines, as British Honduras is on an important secondary route through Central America.

Liverpool to Belize, 4,700 miles, is a 20-hour plane trip away – 13 hours in the air. In a BOAC plane, leaving London's Heathrow Airport at four o'clock in the afternoon, one can usually count on arriving in British Honduras at nine the next morning, Belize time. The stop at Miami (eleven o'clock local time) allows for a night's sleep in the Airport Hotel before taking the Tan Airlines plane. From Miami one flies south-west first – across a lake in Florida with a view of the causeway over the coastal islands of Key West. Then, onward over the Gulf of Mexico, over Cozumel, and south, down the coast of the State of Quintana Roo in Mexico.

The land here appears half drowned, as if Noah's flood had never properly receded. Islands lie scattered in a sea of light green. There are elongated estuaries, more swamps than are believable, and islets so small that they can barely support a solitary palm. The Spaniards did not colonize this coast. It remained a wilderness until the twentieth century, when those coral islands were considered perfect spots for relaxing millionaires.

The approach to Belize International Airport is a featureless landscape of scrub and trees to match. Passengers step out into a sweltering atmosphere and shed coats and ties as they move through the haze of the asphalt apron. All around is flat, wet ground, scantily covered with reedy plants. Near the airport building a couple of palm trees are mirrored in shallow pools of water, and further relief is provided by the sight of hedges of hibiscus. The hibiscus is used for hedges as easily as privet is in London's suburbs. The flowers, in sizes from a saucer to a soup-plate, are red, pink, yellow or striped and with plain or frilled petals. Sometimes a gardener will indulge himself in the fantasy of grafting buds of different varieties on to a common stem, producing a bush with flowers of several colours.

At the airport the rumble and clatter of earthmoving machines are the outward signs of the planning of new runways for the use of modern aircraft. From here runs a ten-mile road across a swamp to the city. On the trip into town we stopped near the bridge over the Belize River. The ground beside the road squelched and black water oozed over the edges of our shoes. The vegetation that had solid stems consisted of sharp, four-inch long thorns, some curved like fishhooks; those that were not thorny had hollow stalks filled with ants. One look was enough to satisfy scientific curiosity. Mangroves lined the banks of the river, and in that saturated world the only signs of life were the egrets and herons on the trees. Like so many silt-laden rivers, the Belize stream is building a delta out to sea. Geologists say that once upon a time the site of London was also a tropical swamp.

The territory of British Honduras forms the eastern edge of a vast continental block of limestone. It began perhaps a hundred million years ago when a shallow sea extended over the middle of the Atlantic Ocean. The limestone stretches from Yucatán in the north to Nicaragua in the south, over 800 miles long, and from east to west the greatest distance is 400 miles. It is not distorted or folded, but slightly tilted. The western and southern parts have been forced up some thousands of feet; the elevation continues at the rate of about a foot in 1,000 years. The gross rate is greater, but erosion rapidly takes place under the tropical rainfall, and the surface is cut into deep ravines. This is, I believe, the origin of the Spanish name; for 'Honduras' means in that language 'the depths' and refers to the deep valleys that criss-cross the Republic of Honduras to the south.

The tilting of the land has tipped the eastern edge under shallow water, causing the continental shelf to continue into the Caribbean Sea for 20 miles. Here is the second longest coral reef in the world, surpassed only by the Great Barrier Reef of Queensland. The innumerable cays are those portions of the reef which protrude above the surface.

Cay is pronounced 'key', and farther up north in Florida the spelling has become key. The word is a corruption of the Spanish 'cayo', meaning a beach, sandbank or islet. Thus Cayo Hueso, Bone Beach, so named from the skeletons of some unfortunate people who perished on the sand, has become Key West.

In comparatively recent geological history, despite the continual elevation of the land, a marine transgression has taken place; the sea level is higher than it was a few thousand years ago. A large part of the area of British Honduras is overlaid with alluvial deposits and beds of sand that rise in ridges.

The peninsula of Yucatán is flat, and the dullness of the landscape continues into the north-western part of British Honduras. Here cultivation is to be found: sugar plantations and valleys worked by the Mennonites. The greater part of the terrain is overgrown with bush, ridges of sand, and pines, contrasting with the lusher vegetation of the wet southern parts, where in bygone years they cut precious logwood. In the eighteenth century this wood fetched the fabulous price of £100 a ton.

Some farming is carried out in the centre of the country and cattle ranches have been established. Of recent years the urge

3

to own citrus plantations has made some merchants of Belize City invest their surpluses in agricultural real estate. However, the big plantations of citrus fruit are farther south, centring on the port of Stann Creek. Most of the orchards belong to two large companies, but there is an increasing number of smaller growers, who supply the big plants with grapefruit and oranges.

The elevation of the southern parts of British Honduras culminates in the massif of the Maya mountains. An outlying ridge to the north-east of these heights, clothed with dense tropical forest, forms a line of crests, the Cockscomb Range. Between their foothills and the sea the mangrove swamps stretch to Lake Izabal in Guatemala. In the mountains, a sparse population of Kekchi Indians cultivate their milpas – fields under shifting cultivation in which they grow maize, beans, cassava and plantains. Along the coast there is a sprinkling of people of very diverse racial origins; the majority are known as Caribs. Apart from Stann Creek Town and Punta Gorda there are no settlements in this district large enough to be termed towns.

San Ignacio (formerly El Cayo) is 72 miles inland from Belize City along the Western Highway, and Benque Viejo del Carmen is another 10 miles farther west.

As the names indicate, they were founded by Spanish-speaking people; Spanish is spoken by most of, and understood by all, the people there. Several thousand Maya Indians live in this part of British Honduras. A fairly large number of people come in from Petén in the adjoining part of Guatemala to do their marketing. The frontier, completely open and unmarked, has one Customs point where the road from Belize ends on the frontier of Petén.

No other river equals the size of the Belize in British Honduras. Its head lies in the rain-forest of Petén. Numerous tributaries join the river as it flows into the Caribbean, five miles from the capital city. While its lower reaches are sluggish, often brimming over in its meandering through the swamps, the upper reaches are swift and the water surges through ravines, over boulders and rapids.

Between the Hondo, the main river in the north, and the Belize River, runs the New River. Along this come the tree trunks felled by lumbermen; they are bound into rafts on the coast near Orange Walk Town and towed to sawmills at Belize

4

City. The principal towns here are Corozal Town and Orange Walk Town. Across the Hondo is the City of Chetumal in the State of Quintana Roo. Here a road is being continually improved from Mérida in the north of Yucatán down to Chetumal, so that adventurous tourists can arrive in Belize City on their own wheels, somewhat battered but triumphant.

A good road runs westwards from Belize City to Benque Viejo del Carmen on the frontier with Guatemala, with a good connection to Stann Creek. From Stann Creek Town there is also a fair weather road going south to Punta Gorda, although all traffic goes by coastal boats. The largest of these boats can carry 35 tons of cargo, and as many passengers as can squeeze in sideways.

2. EARLY HISTORY

BRITISH Honduras is not known by this name to the neighbouring countries in Central America. They call it 'Belice' (Belize in English), pronounced as three syllables. The name of British Honduras dates from a proclamation in 1840 and the title was only adopted officially when the territory became a Crown Colony in 1862. It was invented in London, to distinguish that part of the east coast of Central America which, by treaty with the United States of America, remained under the British flag after the rest was relinquished to 'Spanish Honduras'.

The name 'Belice' referred at first to the river, then to the town that grew up on the delta, and now applies to the hinterland. The first mention of the name can be traced to a Dominican friar, José Delgado, who in 1677 travelled from Guatemala to Mérida in Yucatán. He went north up the coast, and mentioned the names of the rivers he had to cross. The land was sparsely inhabited by Maya Indians, probably semi-nomadic, moving from place to place as they exhausted the soil with their primitive agriculture. The Mayan names have mostly been replaced by English, but three rivers are recognizable. Fray Delgado's Rio Soyte has become the Sittee River, and the Xibum is now the Sibun. Next to the Sibun he mentioned the Balis. It is also recorded by this traveller that he met with a party of English on the Manatee River, and they despoiled him of his clothes and his servant, leaving him naked on the beach.

The name Belize probably has an Indian origin. The second syllable seems to be the well-known Mayan, Itzá, still a surname among the Indians in Yucatán. A local poet has coined 'Balitza', just as we might say Britannia for Britain. The real derivation was obscured by the impingement of the Scottish surname, Wallace. Central Americans, speaking Spanish, which has no W sound, pronounce a W as V, and do not distinguish between V and B, which they pronounce exactly alike. Therefore, we find in Spanish documents the forms Balis and Walis; sometimes the same person will use both spellings. This gave rise to the theory that Belize is a derivation from Wallace. As an alternative, someone found a French word 'balise', meaning a lighthouse or beacon, and supposed that there was a beacon at the mouth of the river and that the stream was named from that. Probably the original name was 'the establishment of Wallace at Belize', for the expression 'el establecimiento de Walis a Belice' does occur in Spanish documents.

This Wallace is a legendary character about whom nothing much is really known. It is said that he was a lieutenant of Sir Walter Raleigh. The Archives of British Honduras contain the following information. The Honduras Almanack for 1826, the first officially authorized historical report of the Colony, states that the settlement is not older than about 1650, when it was used as a refuge from the Spaniards. In the 1829 Almanack, however, the first British settlement was stated to have been made by shipwrecked sailors in 1638. In the 1827 Almanack the credit for discovering the mouth of the Belize River and making it his place of retreat is given to Wallace, a lieutenant among the buccaneers, from whose name 'Belize' is said to be derived. The 1839 Almanack gives the founder as the Scottish Corsair chief, Wallace, a native of Falkland in Kinross-shire, who after being driven from Tortuga, erected huts and a fortalice at the spot called after him by the Spaniards 'Wallis' or 'Balis'.

Bridges, in his *Annals of Jamaica*, states that Willis, the notorious buccaneer and ex-governor of Tortuga, was the first Englishman to settle on the river, to which he gave his name. He dates this 1638, the year in which the Spaniards drove the buccaneers out of Tortuga. Bancroft, in a *History of Central America*, gives Peter Wallace with 80 men as the first settlers at Belize River. And finally, Asturias, a Guatemalan historian, states that the settlement was founded by Wallace, formerly Raleigh's First Lieutenant and right-hand man, who, he says, is supposed to have first reached Belize in 1617. Asturias, however, quoting Spanish authorities, says that Wallace left England for America on 14th May, 1603, with six ships, and believes that he then founded the settlement, remaining as its leader.

From this slender store of tales and suppositions have been concocted tales of piratical frays, which are as entertaining as they are improbable. That the Belize River was a lair of pirates is most unlikely, for they had far better lurking places among the cays. The French and the Dutch seem to have preceded the English and Scots. The Turneffe Islands, out on the barrier reef 25 miles east of Belize City, owe the name to the French 'Terre Neuve'. A local historian of British Honduras, Mr. E. O. Winzerling, claims that a Dutch captain, Cornelius Jol, visited these islands regularly after 1627 and gave Dutch names to those he frequented, such as Cay Bokel, from the bend or buckle of the Turneffe group.

The truth is that we have no firm ground until 1655, when disbanded English sailors and soldiers came from Jamaica. The band of heretical interlopers who maltreated Fray José Delgado in 1677 may have been a remnant of these. Whether there ever was a Wallace cannot be proved. He may have been one of the Jamaican emigrants of 1655, who were not buccaneers or pirates, but simple lumbermen with a purely commercial purpose. Piracy does not seem to have been the occupation of British settlers on the coast at any time. They were mainly interested in mahogany for shipbuilding and repair work. The logwood trade boomed as textile exports from England rose at the end of the seventeenth century, for from logwood was obtained the best dye for cloth.

No permanent settlement was established for many years. There were seasonal activities, as the logs accumulated along the river banks and awaited the arrival of the ships that would take them to England. These voyages were organized by the merchants of Port Royal and Kingston in Jamaica. It was not until well into the eighteenth century that the provisional camps of the loggers began to be occupied all the year round. The people in these villages were negroes and Scots, who felt no allegiance to the Spanish Crown; they paid no attention to the Spanish officials who occasionally visited them to confirm overlordship.

Settlements spread along the coast, from the western side of the peninsula around Yucatán, along the north-facing coast of what is now the Republic of Honduras, and down the east coast of Nicaragua. The islands of the Bay were settled by people of English speech and mixed blood, mainly Scottish and negro; those islands, of which Roatán is the largest, are still English speaking, although politically they are part of the Republic of Honduras.

The Spaniards considered that the English had no right

to be there. The argument was endless, for each side ignored the reasons given by the other. Queen Elizabeth I, in a letter of 1587 to her brother-in-law, King Philip II of Spain, rebuked that monarch for presumption. He had complained officially about English interlopers in Spanish-American waters and the disregard by these robbers of his sovereignty, which had been confirmed by the Pope. The Queen rapped her fellow monarch over the knuckles, as if she were his governess. She denied that the Pope had any authority, and much less prerogative, to divide up America; she acidly pointed out that to have discovered a coast and to have named a cape or a river, without having established a settlement, gave no claim to jurisdiction. Possession was nine points of the law, and King Philip merely waved useless title deeds in her face. In the succeeding centuries some reciprocal arrangements were hammered out. London did not deny, and Madrid did not renounce, Spanish sovereignty over the east coast of Central America; but the loggers paid no attention to the treaties. In fact, the question of peace or war lay with the Spanish Governor of Yucatán; if he were an energetic man he would evict the loggers; if he were easy-going or apprehensive of the extension of the fighting he would leave them in peace.

In these circumstances, the loggers, known as Baymen, became permanent settlers and gradually were conceded permission to cut logs in between intermittent periods of active persecution. When too hard pressed they called on the English authorities to avenge them, and at times they were protected by naval operations. When England and Spain were at war, the loggers had ample support. They numbered several hundred at the beginning of the eighteenth century, and elected among themselves seven magistrates to decide quarrels and administer justice in a rough and ready way. A 'Superintendent', Henry Sharp, was appointed by the inhabitants and is mentioned in 1738 as the chief magistrate; but he had no real authority over the others, and his was probably only a courtesy title.

No code of laws was promulgated until the year 1765, when Sir William Burnaby, Commander of the British squadron at Jamaica, arrived with Captain James Cook at Belize to give protection against the Spaniards. Burnaby organized the Baymen politically and codified the 'Ancient Usages and Customs

9

of the Settlement' into what was known as 'Burnaby's Code'. He also suggested to London that a Superintendent be appointed by the Crown, as he found the inhabitants to be 'in a state of anarchy and confusion'. An official Superintendent was finally appointed in 1784. He was an Irishman, Edward Marcus Despard. He took up his duties in 1786, returned in 1790, disgruntled, and was dismissed in 1791. He went back to Ireland and there conspired to assassinate King George III and to establish a republic, and for that he was hanged in 1803.

It is not recorded whether the codification of laws and customs in Belize by Admiral Burnaby was noticed by the Spaniards. It is possible, however, that some inkling of what was afoot did reach them for in a few years they reacted vigorously.

On a coral islet, known as St. George's Cay, a place surrounded by reefs and mangroves, freed of mosquitoes by the sea breezes, a settlement of Scots and negroes grew up, and showed signs of becoming a regular port of call. It was advantageously situated between the northern tip of Yucatán and the Isthmus of Panama, within easy reach of Jamaica. It was defended by shoals provided by nature, and ships provided by Glasgow. In 1779, the governor of Yucatán organized an expedition which ended in the capture of the settlement. Some of the settlers escaped southwards and westwards to the Belize River swamps. Others were taken prisoner and marched 300 miles along the length of the Yucatán peninsula to captivity in the town of Mérida. Many of them did not survive the hardships of the trek. The cruelty shown here had been exceptional, for the Spanish authorities, despite provocation, had hitherto been forbearing. Resentment against the Spaniards flared up in all the logging camps, and St. George's Cay was reoccupied with defiant gestures.

It would seem that at that time the site of the present Belize City was not occupied. The records mention a meeting of the inhabitants on 10th April, 1765, the same year as that of Burnaby's visit to 'Kaye Casine'. (The Spanish name for St. George's Cay was originally Cayo Cocina – Kitchen Island.) Other public meetings were held there later, but not until 1784 do we read of meetings held at 'Belize Rivermouth', or at the 'Court House, Belize Point'. After the first superintendent arrived he lived at a fort erected on the site of the abutment of the present road-bridge over the Belize River, where some cannon were dug up in the 1930s. The physical features of the mouth of the Haulover Creek were different 200 years ago. Most of the city is built on reclaimed land, and where the houses are now there was probably wet mangrove. Islands of silt are continually built up as the river's delta spreads farther out to sea. These were the swamps in which the survivors of the Spanish assault on St. George's Cay took refuge; it can be surmised that the foundation of Belize as a city dates from that unfortunate episode.

The appointment of a Superintendent by the British Government was an assumption of sovereignty. The Baymen had no use for the King of Spain and his subordinates. They went about their business, recognizing no overlordship except that of the British Crown, and they were always loyal. The Spanish point of view was that the Baymen had only a concession to cut timber in the possessions of the King of Spain, and had no permission to establish permanent settlements. This was the reason for the Spanish expeditions of 1718, 1724, 1733, 1747, 1751, 1754 and 1778; their object was to expel the intruders neck and crop. After 1779 an inevitable duality came into being. Though formal acknowledgment was made of Spanish sovereignty, the

Sports fishermen catch a wide variety – marlin, king mackerel, sailfish, barracuda, bonefish and snook.

British did what they liked in the Bay of Honduras. Treaties in 1783 and 1786 confirmed the *status quo ante*, leaving the Baymen at Belize on Spanish soil. The pretence of actual sovereignty had by then become transparently thin – disregarded by all the English speaking inhabitants; even the Spaniards began to cede. They began to speak of a 'lease' of Belize to the Baymen, and a lease was considerably more than a mere concession to cut timber. It implied accepted occupation. Some change in the legal status of the settlement was obviously around the corner.

The Superintendent, after Despard, was Colonel Peter Hunter, who assumed office in May 1790. This energetic officer had no use for the hair-splittings of diplomacy. Although Lord Grenville in London had declared that there was no intention of setting up 'anything resembling Colonial government' in Belize, Colonel Hunter immediately started to fortify the town. He formed a corps of volunteers, gave them arms, and established a service of spies who reported to him exact news of the Spaniards' movements. To prevent secrets leaking out he published a regulation against enticing negro slaves from the settlement. In an attempt to cripple the operations of the loggers the authorities of Yucatán had adopted the plan of persuading the slaves to run away in order to leave the Baymen with no labour force. The punishment decreed was 13 lashes applied on three separate days, and to have the right ear cut off. The records do not reveal that any delinquent slave earned for himself this rigorous correction.

After a year of organization Colonel Hunter went back in the spring of 1791, and for the next six years seven elected magistrates ran the affairs of the Baymen of Belize. In 1796 war broke out again between Britain and Spain.

The imminence of the conflict between Britain and Spain was known to the settlers at Belize River, causing them much concern. Relations with the Spanish governor of Yucatán were reasonably cordial. There was, in May 1796, a Spanish commissary at Belize River negotiating with the magistrates of the settlement the interminable cases of fugitive slaves from Spanish territories to Belize, and from Belize to Spanish lands. The Commissary, a Juan O'Sullivan, of Irish descent, was no doubt gathering military intelligence as well. The magistrates wrote in March 1796 to Rear Admiral William Parker of the British naval

forces based on Jamaica, informing him of the warlike prepara-
tions of the Spaniards. The Admiral sent a small ship under the
command of Captain Guerin to visit the settlement and report.
In October of that year the magistrates thanked Governor
Balcarres of Jamaica for the gunpowder and small arms sent in
the Kingston schooner, but lamented that their position was
hopeless. They declared themselves surrounded by Spaniards
and unable to defend themselves. Their commerce was injured
by the French war and their treasury was empty, as they had
spent their money on the necessaries of life – purchased at
profiteering prices from speculators. They were divided in their
opinions on what should be done. Some wanted to resist but
others were for abandoning the settlement and taking their
families to Jamaica.

The salvation of the settlement owes as much to the energetic
steps of Governor Balcarres in Jamaica as to any other man.
In December 1796 he appointed Major Thomas Barrow as
Lieutenant-Colonel, to avoid being outranked by Commissary
O'Sullivan, who held that rank in the Spanish army, at a salary
one guinea and a half a day, for himself and his assistant.
According to whether there was peace or war with Spain, Barrow
was to act as Superintendent or Commander-in-Chief. In
this he was acting without specific instructions from Whitehall. Barrow reached the Belize River on 1st January, 1797, and
on the 17th learnt from a captured Spanish officer that war had
been declared on 7th October, 1796; so he published his commission as Commander-in-Chief as well as his appointment as
Superintendent. He began the organization of defence, the men
parading every morning and evening with arms, and a certain
'Mr. Murray' instructed them at drill. A sloop, the *Merlin*, under
Captain Dundass arrived at the settlement with more munitions.
Animated by their example, the Baymen met in public on 1st
June, 1797, and voted, 65 against 51, not to evacuate the settle-
ment.

The year was one of dragging anxiety. Provisions ran short and
despite the valiant resolution of 1st June, Lt.-Col. Barrow was
writing, 10 days later, to Governor Balcarres to say that the
situation in the settlement amounted to absolute anarchy. A few
days later the schooner *Montego Bay*, convoying the transport,
Mary, laden with provisions, came most seasonably to their relief.

The *Mary* contained provisions for 1,000 men for three months. The Governor promised to send the *Brutus*, convoying two more ships, with provisions for 1,000 men for six months. He also announced the sending of 60 men of the 83rd Regiment and three companies of the 2nd Regiment, the Irish Brigade, a total of 200 rank and file. The detachment of the 83rd did not sail in the end, but was replaced by some of the Royal Artillery 'together with some Iron Ordnance of a lighter calibre'. These troops arrived in September with a loss – considered light – of only 23 of the Irish from yellow fever and two artillery men from other illnesses. Sixty-five of the survivors were sick in Belize a month after their arrival.

In January 1798 Balcarres proposed to send officers, non-commissioned officers and drummers of three companies of the 6th West India Regiment to train 171 privates to be provided by the Baymen from their slaves. However, as these men had been withdrawn from military service, he was sending the enlisted men of the 6th West India Regiment who had unanimously volunteered for the expedition. Some Baymen then permitted their slaves to serve again and an equal number of free negroes volunteered. A prominent merchant of Belize, Mr. Thomas Paslow, equipped his own scow as a gunboat, and manned it with his slaves, into whose hands he had no fear of placing weapons. Thomas Potts followed his example. A fleet of improvised gunboats, made of tree trunks chained and spiked together, manned by the loggers, received the heartening names of *Towzer*, *Tickler*, *Teazer*, *Swinger* and *Mermaid*.

The last mention of Captain Dundass of the sloop *Merlin* in the Archives of British Honduras is under the date 2nd May, 1797. We hear no more of that officer, and on 13th June, 1798, Captain Ralph Moss was appointed to the ship. Apart from the *Merlin*, armed with eight 18-pounders and with a crew of 50, Captain Moss recorded the total effectiveness as follows:

2 Sloops with one 18-pounder and 25 men
1 Sloop with one 9-pounder and 25 men
2 Schooners with six 4-pounders and
    25 men each, making 50 men
7 gun flats with one 9-pounder and
    16 men each, making 112 men.

On 3rd September, 1798, the Spanish fleet of 32 vessels – some of which were mere rowboats – manned by 500 sailors and 2,000 troops (according to Colonel Barrow's report, although the Spanish accounts give the total as 3,000), passed Cay Corker, and made for the shoal water of Montego Cay. This movement was foiled by the British squadron, led by the sloop, *Merlin*, in most professional style. On the 5th the Spaniards tried again by a different route, aiming at the occupation of St. George's Cay as their advance base. There was a prodigious amount of gunpowder burnt to no effect, and they were frustrated again. Next day they tried at Long Cay; but Captain Moss with *Merlin* and two of the Belize vessels beat them back by superior handling of his guns, always keeping between the Spaniards and the Cay. A feint was made next day directly at the mouth of the Belize River itself. (Did the Drowned Cays in front of the river not exist then?) The move was correctly interpreted, and the watch on the strategic point of St. George's Cay was never relinquished.

On the 10th the enemy attacked directly against St. George's Cay. As their whole force advanced, the little fleet of Belize – concentrated on the sloop *Merlin* – drew out to meet them, at one-tenth of the enemy's strength. Captain Moss handled his ships with supreme skill, and his science and knowledge were made effective by the support of his men. The negroes went into action with great bravery, cheering as the Spanish shot went over their heads, and they engaged the enemy with spirit. Firing began at half-past two in the afternoon; at half-past three the enemy concentrated on the *Merlin*. Seventeen small craft came to her assistance. An American captain, Osmar, who had volunteered with his ship, distinguished himself. Stranded on a reef, he moved over to a raft, from which he repelled the efforts of five, and afterwards of seven, Spanish gunboats. Colonel Barrow himself hastened to the support of the navy, but by the time he reached the *Merlin* the Spaniards had broken off the engagement and retired. Then night fell. Next morning the enemy were seen sailing away to Bacalar in Yucatán, to the accompaniment of the derisive cheers of the Baymen, both black and white.

The abandonment of the fight by the Spaniards has never been explained. They fought well while the engagement lasted, although they were no match for the professional seamen of the English sloop. That the attack should have been given up so rapidly cannot be laid to cowardice. Perhaps lack of food and water made it imperative to return to the base at Bacalar, which meant that the battle of St. George's Cay had been won by Captain Moss in the days before the general engagement – when he baulked their efforts to land.

Colonel Barrow in his report was very pleased with the slaves who took part. He wrote: 'You will be astonished to hear that our Negro men (who manned the fleets) gave a hearty cheer, and in the midst of a firing of grape kept up upon them from the Spanish vessels . . . those Negroes in an undaunted manner rowed their boats and used every exertion to board the enemy'. Captain Moss of the *Merlin* in his despatch wrote: 'The spirit of the Negro slaves who manned our small crafts was wonderful'.

It was a co-ordinated effort by all members of the community; and the glory belonged as much to the negroes as to their white brothers in arms. Colonel Barrow and Captain Moss recognized this bravery with generous frankness.

To those whose mental picture of slavery in America is coloured by a portrait of humble black virtue tyrannized by a Simon Legree, who enlivens reluctant movements with a big whip, it must seem incredible that an owner in the eighteenth century could entrust arms to his human chattels and move in confidence among them, supported loyally by the very men to whom he denied the first of human rights. But when we examine the circumstances in the Bay of Honduras, the institution of slavery there loses much of its horror. It should be remembered that they were enslaved by people of their own race, who captured them in war. They were sold on the coast of Africa and again as part of a lot on the quayside of Jamaica. They were then bought by the loggers of Belize. That ended their purgatory for they entered into a new life. The Baymen required tall, strong men who could cut down trees three yards thick, and to make good use of these expensive operatives and maintain their strength, they had to be cared for. The camps were surrounded by hundreds of miles of trackless wilderness, into which any recalcitrant slave could vanish, carrying with him equipment difficult and costly to replace. Therefore, it was essential for the Baymen to keep their labour force in good health and spirits and provide them with some inducement to continue in their employment. Furthermore, ill treatment of a crew of hefty lumberjacks armed with large, sharp axes, which they were accustomed to twirl around their heads with ease, would soon make any oppressor a candidate for the chopping block. We find considerable evidence in the annals of Belize to show that rough comradeship existed between black and white; and if the law gave the white man a right to sell the black, it was seldom abused. The negro slaves were mostly content with their work and their condition. They had in fact the best conditions available in that rough age and place. Wages were low, and a free man could not live better than the well treated slave.

Some exceptions could no doubt be found; some cases of negroes fleeing from their work can be counted. The Spanish efforts at enticement must have been at times successful, or Colonel Hunter would not have decreed such a severe deterrent as lashes and mutilation. On the whole, relations between races were excellent. The blacks depended on the whites for employment, food and consumer goods, and for the marketing and finance of the lumber trade, without which both would have disappeared from the coast. The whites depended on the blacks for the cutting of the logs and provided optimum conditions under which the work could be carried out. Therefore, Thomas Paslow could put weapons into the hands of his slaves, and see them cheerfully fight against the Spaniards, who supposedly came to release them from bondage. If we admire the negroes for their spirit, we must also respect the Baymen for their decent treatment. The result was independence from Spanish rule.

On 29th October, 1799, the Baymen declared at a public meeting that 'the tenure and possession of the country is altered. His Majesty holds it by force and it may in some degree be considered as a Conquered Country'. The Union Jack flew over public buildings in Belize, which was from then a British Colony in all but name, in spite of Lord Castlereagh's official declaration, in December 1805, that the settlement was 'within the territory and jurisdiction of a foreign power and therefore not a Colony'. Even as late as February 1809, the magistrates of Belize made a statement about the 'undoubted right of ownership of the Settlement by the King of Spain'. This prompted the superintendent to question their loyalty. He proclaimed that the right of interference in internal affairs was vested solely in the King and Parliament of Great Britain. The magistrates hastened to reassure him of their loyalty.

THE BALLAD OF THE BATTLE OF ST. GEORGE'S CAY COMPOSED IN
BELIZE UNDER THE NAME OF

'The Tenth Day of September'

It was the tenth day of September,
In ninety eight *Anno Domini*,
When our forefathers won the glorious fight –
The Battle of St. George's Cay.

Then cheer them, hail them!
Let our grateful loyal hearts not fail them,
As we march and shout and sing with merry glee:
The Battle of St. George's Cay!

3. POLITICAL DEVELOPMENT

IN the last years of the eighteenth century the Spanish colonial organization began to decay. For over 250 years that system had maintained unity, peace and, according to Spanish ideas, justice, but with the French Revolution came a questioning of preconceived ideas; the bonds that held the mother country to the colonies were loosened. The colonists, called 'criollos' in Spanish, or creoles in French, began to hanker after self-rule and similar innovations.

One of the effects of this stirring was to incline them to trade with heretics, more especially as the industrial revolution in England was flooding the world's markets with desirable consumer goods. This tendency impinged on the life of the loggers of Belize. Until then, the only activity in the Bay of Honduras had been lumber cutting, chiefly logwood for dyeing, since it was, weight for weight, a far more precious commodity than mere mahogany. Now the Baymen became merchants, and Belize developed as the entrepôt between Jamaica and Central America.

At first the old regulations were in force – officially, at least. The demand for English manufactured goods became speedily so great, and the profits in handling them so high, that any risk involved appeared negligible, and any Spanish regulation pettifogging. A flood of contraband entered Central America through the north coast of Honduras, and smuggling enriched unscrupulous traders in Belize. Large warehouses stocked with goods arose at the mouth of the Haulover Creek, and the settlement grew into a city. This development meant that new methods of control and arbitration were required; the political organization of the English-speaking part of Central America had to be overhauled.

The mists of the seventeenth century hide the beginnings of order and law on the Mosquito Coast – fortunately, perhaps, for our susceptibilities. For we can be sure that the prevailing conditions amounted to anarchy. Crimes went unpunished, debts were unpaid; unless the stronger could revenge his wrong and extract payment from his reluctant debtor.

The rearguard of the ancient Mayas was too few in number to preserve any ancestral lore or law. The Indians kept up a few traditional customs and some superstitions, not so much theology as magic and witchcraft.

To that way of life the incoming Baymen, craggy Scots for the most part, with ideas as immovable as the reef itself, were impervious. Contact with the Indians was confined to casual encounters and some trade in lumber, as the felled trees floated down the rivers. The English-speaking newcomers brought the Anglo-Saxon way of life. Their highest political expression was the periodic Public Meeting, the rules being based on the old privateers' code, which was not fixed at first. It was an event, not an institution; but when the loggers numbered some hundreds at the beginning of the eighteenth century, it took shape. While the records show that emancipated slaves could become voting members provided they had the necessary property or financial qualifications, in fact membership became defined as the privilege of free white men of property. Black men and poor whites shared neither the responsibility, nor the advantage.

By 1738, when the Baymen appointed Henry Sharp under the courtesy title of 'Superintendent', the qualifications for membership were: property worth £400; nomination by a member; a minimum of 25 supporting votes at the meeting; British origin and the readiness to swear that one was ready to fulfil one's duties. Once elected, a member was member for life.

From the members of the Public Meeting, who might number 50, were chosen seven prominent merchants as magistrates. They had no written code of laws; no definite duties fixed by legislation; they functioned as arbitrators rather than judges. The customs that directed their conduct were subject to individual interpretation, and their justice was of a very rough and ready kind. The basis of their procedure was what might be remembered or experienced of Scot Laws of the seventeenth century. Punishments must have included hanging, ear-cropping, whipping and branding on the hand, according to the manners of that age; the annals of British Honduras do not give us details of the execution of this frontier law. In civil cases the magistrate would be motivated by equity only, without any statute book on which to base his decision.

This state of affairs led to much friction and, in 1765, required more experienced and educated direction. England was at war with Spain. As the Governor of Yucatán was again threatening to apply antiseptic measures to this ulcer in the domains of his monarch, the British Government provided protection. It came in the form of a squadron of ships from Jamaica under Rear Admiral Sir William Burnaby. He consulted with the oldest of the Baymen, inquired into their ways and customs, and then called a meeting of the white settlers. He presented in writing what he called: 'The Ancient Usages and Customs of the Settlement'. It was an excellent system for the time and place, organically developed from long accepted custom, and was expressed in simple terms. It became known as 'Burnaby's Code', which lasted as the law of the Bay of Honduras until 1840.

Admiral Burnaby's Code was in brief:
1. No swearing and profane cursing, penalty half a crown fine.
2. No theft allowed.
3. No enticing seamen to abandon ship.
4. No hiring servants without a written agreement.
5. No kidnapping, i.e. press gang methods of recruiting, except for pilots for one trip only.
6. Taxes to be imposed by elected representatives.
7. Courts of Justice to be seven elected magistrates and 13 jurors, all housekeepers.
8. In emergency the authority of the commander of a warship in the Bay should take precedence.
9. Disputes as to interpretation to be submitted to an abitration panel of seven.
10. Crimes not specified to be punished according to custom.
11. Future legislation to be approved by a majority vote of the inhabitants.
12. No distraint on property without a magistrate's order.

This touched the surface of human problems, but it touched on just those problems that presented themselves most frequently in the Bay of Honduras. We must remember that it was made for eighteenth century Scots, who in their own land accepted the stenches of Auld Reekie and the sewage of the Fleet Ditch as normal conditions of residence, even in capital cities.

The defect of Burnaby's Code was that no executive power was

c

provided and the implementation of the code was not possible without some armed force behind it. The Admiral retired after promulgating his laws, and returned a few months later to find the settlement once again in a state of anarchy and confusion. He realized that there was need for a higher political direction. He therefore suggested to London that an Official Superintendent be nominated by the British Government to supersede the elected magistrates. Naturally the authority of the Official Superintendent could not rest on so flimsy a foundation as the co-operation of the Baymen; a force of regular soldiers would have to back him up.

By the end of the century the shape of things to come was definitely emerging. The capital of the settlement was at Belize on the Haulover Creek, not on the main river, and St. George's Cay had become merely an historical site. The Public Meeting which had met there at first now came together in Belize City under the protection and supervision of a Superintendent, supported by a company of British troops. The sovereignty of the King of Spain was rejected completely. Not even the Spaniards attempted to assert it now. The Superintendent was by no means a despot whose word was accepted unquestioned. The Baymen often fought him stubbornly. As they had the privilege of paying his salary and providing the funds for administration, they used these levers to persuade the representative of King George III to come to heel. There was much bickering. Still, administration evolved with the changed times. In 1817 the militia was founded, the origin of the British Honduras Volunteer Guard. In 1819 the Criminal Court was established at Belize by Act of Parliament, and in 1820 the Supreme Court held its first session. Meanwhile, the hinterland of the settlement underwent profound changes.

The final blow to the Spanish Colonial Empire was given by Napoleon in 1808, when his army invaded Spain, dethroned the luckless descendant of Louis XIV and installed his brother as King. The Royal domains in America were left headless. They did not immediately declare for republican government. The Spanish American lands were kingdoms, like Aragón and León and Castilla, federated under the Bourbon crown. Mexico was 'New Spain', and Central America was 'el reino de Goahtemalan' – the kingdom of Guatemala, which extended from Mexico to Panama. The first tendency was to consider that an interregnum existed. Ancient Spanish laws provided that in such a case the authority of the municipalities should rule until a new monarch was proclaimed. However, this admirable solution did not appeal to the temper of the times. With the example of France and of the United States of America before them, the Spanish Creoles decided on the republican system, to the total exclusion of any monarchical system. Having executed by firing squad General Agustín Iturbide, who had declared himself Emperor of Mexico in 1821, they set up imitations of the United States federal government.

Long before this happened the laws restricting trade with foreigners had fallen into disuse. English manufactured articles were in great demand in Central America, so Belize proceeded to supply them. The entrepôt trade flourished for a score of years, greatly to the enrichment of the four or five firms based in Belize. Of these, in the first quarter of the nineteenth century, a certain Mr. Marshall Bennett was the foremost and the most unscrupulous and successful. Administration in Belize had to be adapted to these new factors. Trade was booming. In 1824, Mr. G. A. Thompson, the British representative sent from London to Guatemala to make contact with the new republic, calculated that Belize was exporting commodities to Central America to the value of £1,600,000 and buying from that area goods worth £1,700,000 yearly.

Operations were no longer restricted to the cutting of timber. Agriculture started with the planting of sugar cane to produce rum. The juice was extracted in crude mills with vertical rollers of hard wood, the motive power being supplied by oxen. This had its repercussion at Belize, where a class of shopkeepers was created distinct from the wholesalers of the entrepôt trade. Life in the settlement became far more complicated than it had been in the eighteenth century.

However effective, in theory, might be the spectacle of a Public Meeting and the election of Magistrates by its members, in practice this simple form of government by rugged citizens began to fall behind the needs of the community. By the early nineteenth century membership of the Public Meeting was around 50 or 60 white British settlers, but it varied, because it was self-perpetuating. In 1820 the Public Meeting decided that qualifications for membership, which had been in force for about 100 years, should be altered to 12 months' residence and the owning of property worth £500 in Jamaica currency for white British born subjects, and a property qualification of £1,000, Jamaica currency, for coloured British subjects born in the Settlement, a stipulation which must fairly certainly have ensured their exclusion.

However, it shows that negroes and mulattoes in Belize were engaged in commerce and capable of accumulating capital. That they should be mentioned at all as possible candidates is itself remarkable.

The Public Meetings began to split into factions. They were not political parties of opposed ideologies, such as Whigs and Tories, but represented the personal followings of certain prominent men with a talent for intrigue. We have seen how Admiral Burnaby found after his short absence that, although he had reduced their laws to writing, the Baymen's affairs collapsed into confusion, and to remedy that state of affairs he had recommended the appointment of a Superintendent from London. Even then harmony could not be implanted. Every logger was

Fishing boats in Belize Harbour.

determined to get the maximum advantage for himself with no renunciation of privilege *pro bono publico*. The lumbermen were at loggerheads with the wholesalers and the wholesalers were apprehensive that the retailers might encroach on their business. Elections of magistrates became more and more difficult, and as onerous was the task of the elected magistrate to enforce authority.

A solution was found in 1830, when the Superintendent curtailed the powers of the Public Meeting by introducing legislation by proclamation and, in 1832, personally assumed the right to appoint magistrates. This astounding usurpation of the rights of free citizens was not unpleasing to the inhabitants of Belize. They acquiesced in the measures, which were softened by the creation of an Executive Council, consisting of the Superintendent and the magistrates whom he had appointed. This had the appearance of sharing authority and of streamlining public business. The magistrates had the co-operation of the Superintendent, who could restrain their more self-interested moves, and both were supported by a detachment of the West India Regiment.

In 1841 the Public Meeting petitioned London against legislation by proclamation. London agreed, authorizing the Public Meeting to exercise legislative powers, but offset this by appointing a Colonial Secretary to assist the Superintendent, who now had more detail on his hands than he could conveniently manage alone. Executive Council and Legislature were exhorted to harmonize their goals. The Superintendent ceased to appoint magistrates, who lost their position on the Council, which in 1849 became a purely official body, consisting of the Superintendent, the Chief Justice, the Attorney-General, the Colonial Secretary and the Public Treasurer.

In 1851 the Public Meeting appointed their Chairman, Mr. Coffin, to go to London and petition for confirmation by the Crown of the local legislature, and by an Act of Parliament to confirm their institutions. The result was an Act for a new constitution, passed by the Public Meeting in January 1853, and later approved by the British Government. Burnaby's Code was discontinued in 1840 and replaced by British Common Law. Now the Public Meeting was replaced by a Legislative Assembly of 18 elected and three official members. In the same year the Executive Council was reorganized. The Chief Justice was excluded, as the Executive and the Judicature must be separate in democratic theory, and he was replaced by the officer in command of the troops. Three nominated members were allowed now, but they were appointed by the Superintendent.

All these manoeuvres were natural political phases of a developing community. The people of Belize could be thankful that they had experienced and magnanimous men from London in the chief positions of executive authority. They escaped the century of revolution, dictatorship, massacre and robbery that racked the infant nations of Central America with all the political horrors that unbridled republicanism can evoke.

They made their own laws; but the powers of the Official Superintendent to initiate, amend, assent, and reserve bills for the Royal Pleasure, amounting in practice to a veto, were absolutely necessary as a rein on the excesses engendered by private desires overriding general interest. Even 100 years later this would have been an advanced constitution for a dependent territory; yet within a few years the people threw away their jealously guarded freedom, and committed political suicide.

In 1862 the settlers at last persuaded the British Government to declare the settlement a British Colony, replacing the Superintendent by a Lieutenant-Governor, subordinate to the Governor of Jamaica. This eliminated the last vestiges of self-government in Belize, and in 1871, as a result of a petition to the Queen, the status of the territory was changed to that of Crown Colony.

The reasons for this voluntary repudiation of home rule are obscure; but it was thought at the time that the various factions in the Assembly preferred any master rather than each other. It seems that the elected members formed themselves into cliques, representing various interests, such as the landowners, the commercial houses and the shopkeepers. These interests had their henchmen in the Assembly, and as this or that interest was numerically strongest at any given time, so surely did the Assembly adjust the burden of taxation. In short, there was a state of perpetual discord. Eventually the various interests decided that, rather than be at the mercy of each other, they would prefer to hand over the ultimate responsibility to the British Government. 'What's best administered is best.' In retrospect, it can be seen that the change may also have been due to the realization by vested interests that an elected

Assembly would soon be taken over by popular representatives, whereas Crown Colony government might ensure that they, the well-to-do, would be nominated to serve on the Legislative Council, and thus they could protect their own interests. Their backward step was in fact, 'pour mieux sauter'.

In December 1870 the *elected members* of the Assembly passed a local act abrogating their own constitution of 1853, and substituting a Legislative Council composed of members to be nominated by the Queen, who confirmed the Act on 8th February, 1871. This council was composed of five official members and five unofficial, who were named by the Queen, but in practice being nominated by the Lieutenant-Governor. The old Executive Council still functioned and there were no pluralities – nobody served on both councils. In 1884 British Honduras was separated from Jamaica and the Lieutenant-Governor became a full Governor.

In 1890 the inhabitants of Belize were again petitioning the government in London for elected members in the Legislature; but they were chillingly rebuffed by Lord Knutsford, the Secretary of State. 'I have had no hesitation', said His Lordship, 'in arriving at the conclusion that in a Colony on the mainland of America having relations with the neighbouring foreign countries for which the Crown is responsible, and containing only about 400 inhabitants of European descent out of a total of 30,000, it is impossible for Her Majesty's Government to surrender its control over legislation and finance'. The implied rebuke was that the well-to-do in Belize could not be trusted to be impartial in running the country, for this had been very evident in the last 20 years.

In 1891 a People's Committee was formed to further the Colony's political interests. The opportunity came when the legislative Council, from which the unofficial members had resigned, was made up to strength by officials, and it proceeded to pass a number of bills including one amending the Customs tariff. A member of the People's Committee who was asked to pay increased tobacco duty under the newly amended tariff immediately brought a case against the Collector of Customs on the grounds that the Legislative Council was illegally constituted at the time the tariff was amended. The Chief Justice decided in favour of the appellant. Thereupon the Secretary of State authorized the Governor to make concessions to the People's Committee.

The official members were reduced to three, and the unofficial side was increased to five, and thus had a majority of votes. It could not be considered representative government, as the unofficial members were in any case nominated by the Governor.

Matters continued thus until the war of 1914–18 changed the face of the world. The armed forces of British Honduras played an honourable and valiant part; they were stationed in a place even hotter than Central America – the Persian Gulf and Mesopotamia. In November 1921 the Legislative Council agreed that the time had come for amending the existing constitution. In 1923 a Franchise Commission was set up to sound public opinion and to determine the qualifications for candidates if the elective principle were adopted again. The Secretary of State insisted that this would make it necessary to have an official majority and of the unofficial members he would only allow that four of the seven should be selected by popular vote. This was unacceptable to the People's Committee, and so the matter was shelved.

The first sign that an end to the political impasse might be in sight came in an unexpected and indirect way. A devastating hurricane, in 1931, laid Belize City flat and drowned 2,000 people. Reconstruction was impossible without financial help from the British Government and through large private loans from banks to the merchants and property owners of Belize City. The price extracted for this aid was Treasury control over the local finances, and reserve powers for the Governor to enact legislation essential for the well-being of the Colony, or for the fulfilment of its obligations as a member of the British Empire. In 1935 five members of the Legislative Council were elected again by popular vote. Qualifications were much the same as before: literacy, knowledge of English language, three years' residence and an income of £250 or property worth £125; and the candidates had to deposit £25. However, these requirements, taking into account the depreciation of the purchasing power of money between 1869 and 1935, were far more generous than in the time of the former Legislative Assembly.

The British Government was ready to reinstate the pre-1870 state of affairs in the Colony, and after the Belizeans had again demonstrated their loyalty in the war of 1939–45, steps were taken to give a much more responsible part of the work of running the community to the members that composed it. A constitution was adopted in 1954 giving the vote to all British subjects, who were entitled to elect nine members to a Legislative Assembly of 15, and provide six unofficial members from that Assembly to the Executive Council. This foreshadowed a Ministry responsible to a majority in the Legislature on the British parliamentary principle; but the term 'minister' was not yet applied to the elected members in charge of the departments.

In 1961 another step was taken towards gaining internal self-government by elected representation. When the settlement became a colony in 1862 the inhabitants had been mostly illiterate labourers, with an upper crust of graspingly selfish merchants. In 1961 the majority of the inhabitants were literate and capable of taking an intelligent part in their own affairs, and the white merchants were no longer of paramount influence, nor were they so blindly self-centred. There had also entered the territory a large mestizo group from Mexico and a purely Indian minority from Guatemala, which had little impact politically; but their rights had to be zealously protected. Naturally, with better qualifications among the governed, wider participation in the government was logical and just. As the pre-1870 self-government would have failed in 1961, so the 1961 methods would have been disastrous in 1870. Perhaps the most significant difference was the vastly increased participation of the coloured section of the people in the shaping of their own destiny, and the division of that section into two sharply defined and vociferously opposed political parties, such as had never existed in former years.

British Honduras had matured politically and had come of age. In fact, from being a settlement, it was on the way to becoming a nation, and knew it.

The constitution of 1961 provided for an elected Legislative Assembly which nevertheless still contained official and nominated members, and an Executive Council composed of the Governor and two official members, with six ministers chosen from the majority party in the Legislative Assembly. This regime continued to function until 1964 when, the people of British Honduras having shown that they were politically mature and perfectly able to run their own affairs, a new constitution came into force. Under this the people of British Honduras are governed today.

The Legislature, which is known as the National Assembly, now consists of two chambers; the House of Representatives, composed of 18 members elected by universal adult suffrage, and the Senate, which is composed of eight members appointed by the Governor, five on the advice of the leader of the majority party in the House, two on the advice of the leader of the Opposition, and one after consulting such persons as the Governor considers appropriate. The Senate may suggest amendments to or delay the passing of Bills, but their powers over money Bills are limited.

No Executive Council now exists. It has been replaced by a Cabinet of ministers drawn from the majority party in the House of Representatives and headed by their leader, who has the title of Premier.

The Governor continues to be appointed by the Queen on the advice of the United Kingdom ministers, and holds office during Her Majesty's pleasure.

The Governor's executive and legislative powers have been substantially reduced. His power of requiring legislation to be passed is restricted to measures necessary in the exercise of his special responsibilities. Similarly, in assenting to, or withholding assent from, Bills he is required to act on ministerial advice, except where the interests of his responsibility requires him to act otherwise. However, he must reserve for Her Majesty's pleasure any Bill which appears to be inconsistent with treaty obligations of Her Majesty's Government, prejudicial to the Royal Prerogative, or repugnant to, or inconsistent with, the British Honduras constitution. Any legislation which appears to injure holders of any British Honduras Government stock issued under the Colonial Stock Act 1900 may be disallowed by Her Majesty.

The Governor's special responsibilities are for defence, external affairs, internal security, and the safeguarding of the terms and conditions of service of public officers.

The political evolution which started with the Public Meeting has now reached the stage where the British Government has recognized that independence is a natural and legitimate aspiration, and is prepared to consider a request for further constitutional advance, whenever an approach is made by the elected representatives of British Honduras.

4. THE MOSQUITO SHORE AND THE GUATEMALAN CLAIM

THE early Superintendents at Belize had to administer an area vastly larger than that of the present Colony of British Honduras. Their jurisdiction covered all the east coast of Central America, including the islands of the Bay of Honduras. These islands situated about 20 miles from the coast of Honduras, are the southernmost cays. Ownership changed several times until they became part of the Republic of Honduras. In the eighteenth and nineteenth centuries they were considered to offer strategic advantages as a naval base – like Bermuda or Malta – and therefore had attracted British interest.

The Central American colonies separated from Spain on 15th September, 1821, and immediately split up into five quarrelsome republics. Under monarchy the area had been the kingdom of Guatemala, but that name was rejected by the southern provinces, which felt a furious antipathy towards their former capital. A federal republic was proposed, and created on paper; but it was largely inoperative because of lack of funds and the impossibility of getting any State to obey the Central Government. After several civil wars, during which the ineffective remedy was tried of exiling whoever was on the losing side, the five States each assumed the title of Republic in 1838, and have remained separate to this day.

These republics were powerless, just as the King of Spain had been, to do anything about the operations of the English on the east coast. The Federal Republic under Manuel José Arce as President, and under Francisco Morazán after him, did not question the independence of 'Belice'; but they never had, after fighting for their presidencies, any time left to define the frontier. Arce and his Senate were in favour of returning fugitive slaves who had fled to Guatemala from their masters in British Honduras; but Congress voted against extradition on the grounds that slavery had been abolished in Central America. It did not vote so on the grounds that 'Belice' was their territory.

31

The British government was not ill-informed nor indifferent about Central America. London was anxious to establish good relations with the Federal Republic, and in 1824 had sent over a preliminary delegate in the person of Mr. G. A. Thompson. Civil war between Arce and Morazán filled the scene with the smoke of conflict, and until Morazán defeated the Conservatives, no negotiations could be carried out. In 1833 some tranquillity and consolidation being apparent, Lord Palmerston appointed Mr. Frederick Chatfield Consul-General to the Central American Federation. His instructions were to negotiate a commercial treaty and to deal with the status of Belize. It was a difficult mission to carry out.

Frederick Chatfield has probably been forgotten in England, but not by Central America. He came within an inch of imposing a British protectorate over the isthmus, and to the journalists of Central America he is the prototype imperialist. Chatfield had entered the Guards, but found that expensive career beyond his resources, and so resigned his commission in 1819. Through his aristocratic connections he was able to obtain a minor position in the Consular Service, and served in Aix-la-Chapelle, then part of West Prussia, and at Memel in East Prussia, and at Warsaw.

He was self-confident and aggressive, and frequently exceeded his instructions. He was the possessor of an iron will and of boundless ability and patience. He was an empire builder, when empire building was not only respectable, but meritorious. His photograph, unearthed in Guatemala where the descendants of his friends had preserved a copy, shows a Victorian gentleman with regulation side-whiskers, standing by a pedestal, on which is his stove-pipe hat. He has the air of a man who would brook no opposition, but that may be due to the spirit of the age. We must never forget the background. He was appointed after the Great Reform Bill had succeeded in giving Britain the liberalism that the French Revolution had failed to confer on France. The greatest factor in national thought was the victory of Waterloo. Products of revolution, such as the Central American republics, did not rate very high in his scale of values.

The Colonial Office, being firm on the question of the recognition of British Honduras, provided Chatfield with a draft treaty using the wording: ' . . . places in the possession and occupation of His Britannic Majesty . . .', which left the door open for further expansion. Chatfield arrived at Belize on May 1834, and spent two weeks with the Superintendent, a cultured Scots officer, Colonel Cockburn. He reached Guatemala on 23rd June, 1834, but found no federal authorities. The presidency was vacant, as Morazán had completed his term, and no election for a new president had yet taken place. Chatfield discussed his mission with Marcial Zebadúa, who had been in Europe as representative of the Federal Republic, principally engaged in financial matters. Sr. Zebadúa, an intelligent and patriotic man, warned Chatfield that the Central Americans were extremely sensitive over the sovereignty of 'Belice', and he counselled the utmost tact and caution. His suggestion was that Great Britain should begin talks with a renunciation of any rights over the isles of the Bay of Honduras and the 'Mosquito Shore'.

In August Chatfield managed to have an interview with General Morazán, and they discussed the proposed treaty. 'Belice' was obviously in the hands of British subjects, who would not relinquish an inch of the territory, and who would certainly be supported by the armed might of Britain. Morazán had to fall back on the argument that the British had only a lease of Belize, as the Central American Republic had 'inherited' sovereignty from the King of Spain. He hinted that he might negotiate a treaty with Spain, and settle the sovereignty that way. Chatfield countered with an identical threat – to have a British treaty with Spain in which it would be recognized that Belize was ceded to Great Britain. He insinuated that rejection of his terms, and the consequent failure to implement a treaty, might create the impression that Central America was too insecurely established to be recognized as an independent nation.

This was hard bargaining; but nobody knew better than the president of Central America how insecure the ground was under his feet, and how animosities between the states were undermining the federation. A working agreement was reached, despite the haughty tone of the reciprocal declarations. There was, moreover, a powerful reason for Morazán's 'friendship' with the British envoy. He was trading in his private capacity with Mr. Marshall Bennett of Belize and did not want to destroy a profitable connection. Morazán had received from the government of Honduras a concession to cut timber on the north coast, and had in turn leased that concession to Bennett. If he then were to run the British out of Central America, which a feverish anti-British faction was already demanding, Morazán would have to sacrifice a lot of his profit.

Bennett and a London company promoter, named Thomas Gould, got a concession to cut timber, and to plant English colonists, in the department of Chiquimula and Verapaz in Guatemala, in an area of about 70 miles deep along the frontier with British Honduras. The terms were fantastically favourable. For 1,000 muskets delivered in Guatemala city, and on proof of the settling of the colonists, the land after 20 years was to be their private property. For another 1,000 guns Bennett received a further concession, covering the sites of the present ports of Matías de Galvez and Puerto Barrios on the east coast of Guatemala, where he proposed to set up a rival entrepôt to Belize. Chatfield viewed the development with complacence, as he was sure that the property of British subjects in Guatemala would eventually come under the authority of the Superintendent at Belize. In other words, in due course it would be annexed.

These transactions aroused furious opposition among the people of Central America, and a wave of Anglophobia swept Guatemala. It was claimed that the Belize merchants were sucking the lifeblood of the country, fixing prices low when purchasing and high when selling, so that they were enriching themselves by the ruin of Guatemala. Workmen complained that the cheap English factory goods were driving them out of business, as their cottage industries could not compete. Sr. Mariano Galvez, Chief of State of Guatemala, then found an ingenious way out of the trouble. He made a grant of the land, already contracted to Bennett and his partner, to a local entrepreneur, Juan Galindo, who, despite his Spanish name, claimed to be an Irish born subject of King William IV. It was blandly explained that Galindo's grant was contingent on Bennett's non-fulfilment. If Bennett could not colonize in the stipulated period, then Galindo could take over. Then an uproar was raised by the merchants in Belize. Some of the land granted to Galindo lay within what they considered to be British territory. They declared the concession null and void, and announced that any attempt to implement it would be suppressed with arms. Galindo then had the happiest notion to embroil the United States in the quarrel, and even made a journey to that country and to England to obtain official backing for his claim; but he was not successful.

Consul Chatfield supported Bennett's point of view. In October 1834 he suggested that plenipotentiaries be nominated to negotiate the commercial treaty, on to the ratification of which he proposed to take recognition of British sovereignty over Belize. Galindo received the support of the anti-British element in Guatemala, a powerful party in local politics. They managed to get through the legislature a resolution allowing a two per cent rebate in import duties on goods coming to the Pacific coast ports, that is from other than Belize merchants. Great Britain replied with the threat that Chatfield had made to Morazán. The Duke of Wellington, in June 1835, instructed his Consul in Central America to suspend all conversations regarding the territorial question as negotiations had been opened with Spain.

When Chatfield arrived, the Superintendent at Belize City had been the urbane officer, Colonel Cockburn. In January 1837 he was replaced by Colonel Alexander McDonald, who disdained the petty states of Central America. To King Robert Charles Frederick of the Mosquito nation he awarded equal political status with the chiefs of the state of Guatemala, or any other part of the Federal Republic under General Morazán.

That a distinct human type inhabited the east coast of Nicaragua was a fact. To the Spanish-speaking republicans of the five states of Central America it seemed absurd to claim for the descendants of runaway slaves a political equality with themselves. A few hundred illiterate 'Zambos' – Negro-Indian crossbreeds – whose main occupation was to drink themselves out of existence, could not constitute a state. However, McDonald proclaimed a British Protectorate to shelter these allies of Queen Victoria from the encroachments of Honduras and Nicaragua. He proceeded in this step independently of Consul Chatfield, whose aims were directed towards another goal.

McDonald warned the commandant at the port of Trujillo, on the north coast of Honduras, an officer of the Republic of that name, that he would tolerate no interference with the woodcutters' felling timber in the hinterland. Although Bennett was intimately connected with Chatfield and was one of the factors in the intrigues of the Consul, McDonald forbade him to cut, on the grounds that his permit had been issued by a government that had no legal jurisdiction over the territory in question. The news of these high-handed actions aroused a great wave of anti-British feeling in Guatemala and there were clamours for war with the heretical English.

Chatfield had instructions to co-operate with the military from Belize, and therefore notified the Central American authorities that Great Britain would recognize no concessions that they might make on the Mosquito Coast or in the Bay Islands. In the countless intrigues and counter-intrigues of Central American politics and finance at the time, this was further confusion. Chatfield was forced to support McDonald, over whom he had no control, against the interests of Bennett, for whom he was endeavouring to obtain restitution of losses caused by the troops of General Carrera, who had sacked a farm that Bennett had purchased from the liberal government of that country. This was a property of the Church, which had been expropriated by the Liberals under Morazán, who was the Federal President. Chatfield supported Bennett's claim for $45,875 and presented it to Morazán with an additional $30,000 for loss of profits. Morazán was preparing a campaign against Carrera and needed funds. Chatfield proposed that Bennett should find $11,500 in Belize, $10,000 as a loan to the Federal Government for the purchase of supplies for the campaign, $1,500 to be 'privately distributed'. Bennett was to receive his indemnity in the form of certificates for $85,000 acceptable in the customs houses of Central America as payment of duties on imported goods consigned to him. The scheme fell through as money was not forthcoming from Belize.

Meanwhile Colonel McDonald from Belize was waging a little war of his own. London had come round to his point of view, and was indignant over the insults and injuries offered to the British subjects in the Bay Islands. A sloop was sent from Jamaica, and on 20th April, 1839, hauled down the Central American colours at Port Royal on Roatán. The islanders raised it again; but their minds were made up for them by the colonel, who landed an armed party, hauled down the flag, and arrested five of the ringleaders, whom he shipped unceremoniously to Trujillo on the mainland.

The Guatemalan state authorities retorted by inviting the people of Belize to send delegates to the national constitutional congress in Guatemala, which was to reorganize the state into a republic. By this they claimed sovereignty over British Honduras; but although it was a purely rhetorical gesture, Lord Palmerston took the news very seriously, and declared it was an unfriendly act, and must be immediately rescinded. Rescinded it was, as the alternative would have been war. Chatfield managed to get in touch with Conservatives in Guatemala through a Scots merchant there, George Skinner, as the Guatemalans were coming round to the view that they would like a British guarantee of peace. They were opposed by Morazán, who enjoyed formidable prestige as a winner of battles. Chatfield therefore asked London for permission to give British protection to any state of Central America which might apply for it against any other which did not; but Lord Palmerston would authorize British mediation only if all the states would solicit it jointly.

In London on 15th December, 1840, the decision was taken: ' . . . to impart to a rude and barbarous Race of Men some of the elements of social order, some rudiments of political organization and some instruction in the Truths of Religion . . . to lay a foundation for the Introduction of civilization and Christianity among the Mosquito Nation'. A British force from Jamaica arrived at the port of San Juan in Nicaragua in August 1841, and occupied the place in the name of the King of the Mosquito nation. The commander was Colonel McDonald, and HMS *Tweed* provided the armed might. Lt.-Colonel Manuel Quijano of Nicaragua prepared to resist at first, but capitulated without fighting. He was forced to sign a document in which he appeared to admit that the trouble at San Juan had been caused by his imprudence and was carried off up north to be dumped on shore at Cape Gracias-a-Dios.

The authority of the King of the Mosquito nation was thus firmly established at the mouth of the San Juan River. The real object was to secure the eastern terminus of the proposed transisthmian canal. The act was entirely unauthorized by London, and was carried out wholly on the initiative of Col. McDonald. The impudence of the sally is illustrated by the farce enacted with the tipsy 'King of the Mosquito Nation'. The British members of the expedition were a commission nominated by the Colonial Office, and Lord John Russell had instructed McDonald to disband them. His Majesty, King Frederick of the Mosquito nation, was persuaded, with a liberal supply of rum mixed with the ink of his royal pen, to set up a new commission. This was the same group as the former, now freed from the clogging scruples of Whitehall. The royal signature was obtained to documents which changed the succession to his second son, Clarence, who was a minor, and during his minority the commission was to be a regency board.

In 1844 a British resident was appointed to the Mosquito shore. Chatfield managed to persuade the Chief of State of Costa Rica to send instructions to his minister in London: the request was to be for a British protectorate over that country which was hard pressed by the Republic of Colombia claiming that certain districts on the Atlantic Coast were Colombian territory. The minister refrained from submitting the request to the British Government; he probably changed the destiny of all America by his patriotic action.

However, the best laid plans of Consuls and Colonels go oft awry. In 1848 gold was discovered in California, and a mad rush of United States citizens flooded that state with prospectors. To get there they had either to cross the North American land mass, still a very hazardous and toilsome trek, or sail round Cape Horn. Therefore Central America attracted the eye of Mr. Cornelius Vanderbilt, who was financing railroads. In November 1848, an American Chargé d'Affaires, Mr. Elijah Hise, arrived in Central America, proclaiming the might, protection and republican fervour of his government. His speeches were openly directed against the British Consul. In June 1849, he was replaced by Mr. George Squier, who also went briskly to work. In September he had already concluded a treaty with Nicaragua, in which the right to open a canal was conceded to exclusively American interests, and in October he was negotiating a treaty with Honduras to secure the Pacific terminus in the Bay of Fonseca. In December 1848, he sent a message to the Government of Costa Rica, warning that country that the United States had concluded a treaty with Nicaragua, extinguishing any Costa Rican claims to the San Juan River, and that his country would support Nicaragua to the full. His real target was the British Consul, for whom he had conceived a deadly animosity. It is curious to read Chatfield's pamphlets in which he applies to the American the same words, 'socialist, communist and disorganizer', which the Americans today are so apt to apply to their opponents.

In November 1851, San Juan del Norte, now rechristened Greytown, and occupied by a British resident, was favoured with a visit by Mr. Cornelius Vanderbilt himself; he arrived in a ship called the *Prometheus*. The Mosquito King, represented by the British port factor, demanded dues to the extent of $123. Mr. Vanderbilt refused to pay. But the port factor was supported by a convenient British man-of-war. A round shot across the bows of the *Prometheus*, as she tried to sail away, and another across the stern, with the threat that number three would be a 'bombshell amidships', produced the requested pesos. On his return to the United States the outraged financier started a newspaper war against British Imperialism. The incident was smoothed over; but Lord Palmerston's resignation in December 1851 was at least in part due to the refusal of the British Cabinet to approve of the gunfire.

Backed by the United States the Central American republics became bolder in their language. They poured unwavering scorn on the 'Mosquito Nation', whose interests were said to be at stake, and never would they admit that such a tribe ever existed. They were right; for in the end the British Government abandoned the Mosquito King to his alcoholic fate.

Cooler heads on both sides avoided an armed conflict. Chatfield was recalled and pensioned off, to end his days on Brighton promenade in comfortable prestige. From London Lord Bulwer and from Washington Mr. Clayton discussed differences with understanding and realism. They concluded an agreement, known as the Clayton-Bulwer Treaty, that defined the Central American area as a zone of United States influence. Compensatory allowances were made to Great Britain in other parts. In 1855, another treaty of deeper import was concluded between the two countries. Britain relinquished all but a nominal protectorate over the Mosquito coast, where the sovereignty of Nicaragua was fully acknowledged; on that republic was conferred the privilege of paying an annual pension to the King.

Thus ended a minor episode of national expansion, utterly forgotten by the British public today, but remembered with undiminished bitterness by Central America. To them Chatfield's death occurred only last week. The favourite epithet applied to that diligent servant of British interests is 'El infame Chatfield' – Chatfield the Infamous. Not a year goes by without the newspapers in some Central American country raking up an anecdote about the British Consul-General to the Federal Republic of Central America.

The treaties between the United States and Great Britain had one object – to smooth over the difficulties that had arisen, and to prevent any outbreak of hostilities. The zones of influence that the contracting parties would respect were laid down with precision. Great Britain gave up any claim to any territorial concession on the east coast of Central America south of the Sarstoon River; but in turn was recognized as controlling the stretch of coast northwards from that stream to the River Hondo – in other words, the present limits of British Honduras.

This decision, or award, was accepted by the Central American republics and by Mexico. The nebulous Spanish control over this part of Columbus' discovered continent had been theoretically divided along the River Sibun between the Captaincy General of Yucatán and that of Guatemala. Therefore, Great Britain was holding a piece of land that could have been part of Guatemala, and part of Mexico. To define the western frontier with those two modern states was a routine diplomatic chore.

Under these circumstances Great Britain and Guatemala celebrated a treaty on 13th April, 1859. In the first article Guatemala accepted, as she had always done in practice, the boundaries between Guatemala and British Honduras, and did not concede any territory that previously had been recognized as Guatemalan. Article Seven stipulated that the parties concerned would endeavour to establish adequate communications by road, river or rail, between Guatemala and the Atlantic Coast. There were difficulties of a technical nature in carrying out an agreement for a road to Belize. In 1863 this clause was substituted by an agreement to pay £50,000 to Guatemala, who would take charge of the opening of the road. Great Britain was ready to ratify this codicil; but Guatemala delayed ratification for a year longer, and then began to seek further advantages. At this the British Government refused to ratify, alleging that since the Guatemalan government had not ratified in the duly stipulated period, the *status quo* of 1859 remained in force. Since British engineers had made the preliminary surveys, and money had been spent by the British Government thereon, while Guatemala had done nothing to implement her part of Article

Seven, Great Britain considered that her part had been fulfilled.

So matters remained until 1908, when the Government of Guatemala gave a concession to the International Railway of Central America, then a subsidiary of the United Fruit Company of Boston, Massachusetts, USA, to build a railway from Guatemala City to the Caribbean Coast at Puerto Barrios, 240 kilometres south of Belize. In 1895, Great Britain had offered to hand over the £50,000 to Guatemala to finance a railway through Petén to Belize, but it had not been accepted. In 1934 Britain began work on a road from Belize to Benque Viejo, the most westerly town in British Honduras, on the frontier with Guatemala. It is still the only means of approach by land to that remote district, known as the Department of Petén. This was finished in 1948.

Meanwhile in the 1930s agitation arose in Guatemala about Britain's 'usurpation' of the territory of 'Belice', and the demand was made to 'return' this land to Guatemala immediately and

Maya Indian woman carrying water, San Antonio.

without compensation. To bolster up this claim, Article Seven of the treaty of 1859 was dug up, after having been completely forgotten for 75 years. It was officially given out that this had meant the grant of a territorial concession for the whole of British Honduras, or at least of the part south of the River Sibun, by Guatemala to Great Britain, contingent on the construction of a railway from Belize City through Petén to Guatemala by British money and initiative. In 1963, when the people of British Honduras and the representatives of Great Britain were to meet to discuss internal developments on the political plane, Guatemala demanded to be a party to the discussions, and on being refused broke off diplomatic relations with Great Britain. Also, in one of the frequent revisions of the Constitutions of Guatemala, 'Belice' was described as an integral part of Guatemala, indivisible from the fatherland.

Every offer by Great Britain to submit the disagreement to impartial arbitration, to The Hague Tribunal or any other body that could be relied upon to be sensible, failed against the negative attitude of Guatemala.

Whatever shape the arguments may take, the inherent verity of the claim is quite another thing. The famous Article Seven of the treaty of 1859 is a mere excuse; what prompted the claim in the first place was oil. In the nineteen-thirties there was a rumour that petroleum was to be found in Central America. There was petroleum in Venezuela and petroleum in Mexico, making these countries rich. Perhaps over a huge bowl of oil Mexico and Venezuela were on the rim. Deeper down might there not be a huge reservoir of countless barrelfuls waiting to be found? Did that mean that in the middle, just where Petén and British Honduras languished forgotten, there may be an oilfield?

Oil well drillers came to Guatemala and to British Honduras and applied for permission to sink wells. They spent a lot of money but found no oil. The theory of the oil-soaked syncline of Central America has yet to be proved.

Nevertheless, the Guatemalan claim continues, and has created some odd incidents.

There was, for example, a president of Guatemala, Miguel Ydígoras Fuentes. He had been Ambassador to the Court of St. James and later a political exile in El Salvador; but he was able to make a comeback and was president from 1957 to 1963.

(His great-grandfather was a Spaniard, Marcos Ydígoras, who had been secretary and vice-consul under the 'infamous Chatfield', and had been protected by that functionary against the imposition of forced loans.) In April 1958 President Ydígoras crossed the border of British Honduras, carrying in his hand a copy of the Guatemalan constitution, and with his party presented himself at the Police Station in Benque Viejo. The corporal in charge telephoned his superiors and told them of Ydígoras's request to proceed into 'Belice'. They in turn referred the matter to the Governor, who indicated that General Ydígoras was welcome at any time; but in order to receive him with the style due to his rank, it would be best for him to make some preliminary application. General Ydígoras then retired by the way he had come.

Ydígoras's action would have been considered a defiant gesture by Latin Americans, to whom it was of course directed, but for the existence of a board about 100 yards on the British Honduras side of the frontier. There in Spanish and English (and it should have been in Mayan as well, as most of the Indians there spoke no other tongue) in big black letters on a white background was the notice: 'This is the territory of British Honduras. If you wish to proceed farther into the country, please announce your presence at the Police Station of Benque Viejo, one kilometre farther down this road'. And that is just what General Ydígoras had done, as Mayan Indians did every week-end when they came to market.

In January 1962, Francisco Sagastume, a political opponent of President Ydígoras Fuentes and unsuccessful candidate for the constituency of Petén, arrived with 19 Guatemalan followers and one renegade Belizean at the village of Pueblo Viejo (Old Town), about five miles from the frontier in the very south of the Colony. There he announced that liberation was at hand. On receiving the news 10 of the party discreetly returned to Guatemala in the rain, whilst the leader and the others went on to San Antonio, a small town of about 1,200 people, all Maya Indians. In Pueblo Viejo he had solemnly burned photographs of Queen Elizabeth and the Duke of Edinburgh, together with a Union Jack. Having thus symbolically destroyed the British Empire, he should not have been surprised that the Indians in San Antonio were hostile. Their ancestors had left Guatemala three generations ago to avoid conscription by press gang methods and the forced loans that were then common in Central American politics. The party was requested to leave town, and the local policeman provided them with a truck to do so.

They went to within three miles of Punta Gorda, the administrative capital of the district, and abandoned the vehicle, having run out of petrol. The leader and three others were rounded up the next day by the police of Punta Gorda, which were backed up by a detachment of the Royal Hampshire Regiment. One of the men had already given himself up, and the rest were captured a day later. In March 1962 they were tried in the Stann Creek Town Assizes of the Supreme Court before the Chief Justice. Sagastume and his Belizean accomplice received sentences of 10 years' hard labour. Two of the Guatemalans were bound over to keep the peace and seven were acquitted. The leader and his aide served about nine months of their sentence, and in December 1962 petitioned the Governor of British Honduras for pardon, which was granted.

The prompt movement of troops and the complete serenity of the people of Belize, who made no manifestations outside the Guatemalan Consulate, did not pass unnoticed in Guatemala, where the Government maintained a correct attitude of detachment from the whole affair.

In 1965 a weight-lifting competition for Central America was held in San Salvador, the capital of the republic of El Salvador, and delegates from all Central American countries were invited. There would be the usual formalities, presenting bouquets of flowers to the 'madrinas', raising their country's flag, and playing a few bars of the national anthem as each team came on. It was quite unofficial. El Salvador invited a team from Belize and explained that the national flag and the national anthem were required to complete the event. Belize replied that for lack of a Belizean flag they hoped no objections would be held to raising a Union Jack, and that the music of the proposed Belizean national anthem would be brought over in good time for the band to rehearse. When the team arrived in San Salvador they had brought a Belizean flag as well.

The Guatemalan team refused to admit that 'Belice' was a Central American country, even in an unofficial sporting event. So they announced that if the team from British Honduras competed they would withdraw. The Belize team suggested that the question of their participation should be put to the vote, and this was done. Guatemala and Nicaragua voted to exclude, and Honduras and Costa Rica to include them, while El Salvador did not vote, having indicated very plainly by the invitation that 'Belice' was a country of Central America. If everybody had voted, the result would have been four to two against Guatemala. But Guatemala refused to take part if the British Hondurans were allowed in. The latter were offered a chance to participate as individuals, but declined. As a national team they had been invited, and as such they would participate or not at all, and as spectators to a rather deflated event they remained.

In the Guatemalan claim, the principle of self-determination is completely ignored. Whether the people of British Honduras want to be Guatemalan or not is studiously avoided. On 17th December, 1957, the Legislative Assembly of British Honduras unanimously approved a resolution, rejecting the claim of any government, other than that of the United Kingdom, to sovereignty over British Honduras, declining participation in any plan to incorporate the country in any other, and reiterated their loyalty to the British Crown.

Guatemala maintains a consul in Belize City. The consulate has a flagstaff on which the national flag is raised with the correct protocol. A narrow passage between two shops has a white board at the end with the words: 'Consulado de Guatemala'. Over the shops is the consulate. The consul is eminently a gentleman, as correct and courteous as a consul could be. He has four assistants, which means a lot of work is done. They gather trade statistics, certify documents, issue visas and go through the gamut of work of a consulate. On the office wall there is a map. It shows Belize as a department of Guatemala. The King of England once upon a time claimed to be King of France as well.

45

5. BELIZE CITY AND OTHER TOWNS

THE city and port of Belize stands for the most part on stilts. Concrete bases are laid in the soggy ground and on them rise pillars 10 feet high. Recently someone started to manufacture hollow cement building blocks, but most of the houses continue to be built of wood. This method of building in the air has its conveniences. Ventilation from below gives a more natural cooling than air conditioning. In any case the extreme wetness of the ground makes it necessary to raise the floors.

When the first settlers came to the 'Belize' Point they found a branch of the river running east, forming banks of mud and sand from the silt carried down from the interior. It was named Haulover Creek. On the northern side they set up log houses and straw huts for the slaves. The area was restricted – about 400 yards long and perhaps not 50 yards wide. All around were mangrove swamps and minor channels. Luckily for the Belizeans, they do not have a monsoon climate – months of rain and months perhaps of drought – like other parts of the tropics. The rain provides an adequate supply of drinking water throughout the year; large vats hold the run-off from the roofs.

After the second world war a water supply was built behind the airport, and a six-inch pipe was laid across the swamps to the town. In 1957 another larger pipe was added, and both survived the hurricane of 1961, although some repairs were necessary. Nevertheless, today few houses in Belize City have a piped water supply. It is also still considered advisable to boil drinking water.

In the nineteenth century the south bank of the river was protected by piles, and a wooden bridge was built across the Haulover Creek where it starts to widen. The creek above the bridge was straightened, and the waters were made to run in a man-made channel. On the north bank similar works were undertaken; canals were cut through the back of the town as building began to grow along the original sand bank and spread over the marshes. Log huts began to be replaced by buildings of sawn lumber; some were of brick, which material came from England in the form of ships' ballast. There are still houses on the southern front of Belize City built of yellow brick.

Face the sea, and the south bank will be seen to veer to the right, where shoals and mangroves have formed a few yards out in the bay. Given its natural, unhindered development, the delta would in due course grow farther out to sea, and Belize City would become an inland town.

One of the most intriguing places is Fort George. This section contains the Customs buildings, the Baron Bliss Park, Tomb and Lighthouse, the Fort George Hotel, the Memorial Park and some of the best residential buildings. Forty years ago it was a little swampy island at the mouth of the Haulover Creek.

Fort George got its name in 1803, when a small fort was erected on the little island on the left tip of the estuary. For half a century this fort defended the settlement. The booklet, 'Portrait of a Colony' depicts on its cover Fort George in 1842. The picture shows white and coloured soldiers on duty beside cannon balls and guns, as sailing ships lie in the harbour. Fort George gradually lost its importance as a military defence post after the West India Regiment in the 1850s moved to the Newtown Barracks. It then degenerated into a fishermen's village with a small bridge connecting it to the mainland.

By the 1920s Fort George Island was leased privately. It had

Sergeant's Caye. Men picking conchs on the coral reef. Some conchs – both meat and shell – are exported to a limited market.

coconut trees, and a strait separated it from the town. One went through a lane with the engaging name of Key Hole Alley to get to the bridge. In 1922 the government planned to develop Fort George. A contract was given to the Jefferson Construction Company of the United States. For a sum of $BH300,000,000 the company, between 1922 and 1924, completely filled in the strait, making Fort George Island one with the city. A concrete wall surrounded the island, and a mound at the tip was made with a high groyne to form Memorial Park, in honour of the dead of the first world war. In 1926 Baron Bliss came to Belize City and died on his yacht in the harbour. He left his fortune to the Colony, and his tomb was placed at the point, with a lighthouse beside it. In 1952 the Colonial Development Corporation built the Fort George Hotel on a site reserved for that purpose, and a United Kingdom grant assisted in the construction of the headquarters of the British Honduras Volunteer Guard.

Today Fort George is a busy area; it has the Customs House, the mooring place for coastal boats, and large buildings with offices, including the Mexican Consulate. It is also the section where the doctors and dentists live, and there is a small hospital facing the Memorial Park.

The wide street from the Fort George Hotel runs 200 yards straight to the Marketing Board Building, on the site of the old channel that separated Fort George from the town. The streets have picturesque names. Gabourel Lane curves to the right, and North Front Street to the left. They follow the old shore line, just as Marylebone Lane preserves among London buildings the winding country road that led to the rustic village of St. Mary-le-bourne. A cinema is to be seen there, as well as the showrooms and offices of the principal importers. On the left by the river the Fire Station stands guard opposite the large three-storey Paslow Building, where the Post Office functions on the ground floor. Upstairs are the Ministry of Natural Resources and the Departments of Forestry, Agriculture and Survey.

Opposite the Paslow Building, the swing bridge spans the Haulover Creek. It replaces the old wooden bridge and was a present to the people of Belize from Britain. It provides an exciting game for the little boys of Belize City. Every evening at five a tall policeman and four husky assistants arrive at the bridge with a gigantic key, which is then inserted into a slot in the middle of the bridge. The bridge slowly swings to allow boats to pass up stream to the wharves and warehouses. Pedestrians can continue to cross the bridge while it is swinging open, but inevitably someone has to be last over. He is invariably a small boy who scampers at the last moment past the benevolent policeman's legs. Soon after the bridge is returned to its former position, half the people of Belize City ride their bicycles across to get home for supper.

Across the river from the Fire Station lies the Market Place, an open-sided roofed area. The vistas of plantains and bananas, hanging in bunches from the roof, make a pleasing dash of colour. A favourite fruit in season is the small cherry-like 'craboo', with a yellow skin and penetrating aroma and a small pip inside. As the market is beside the river, its garbage is usually swept into that convenient channel. The moment the scraps fall in the water seems to boil as the catfish fight for the booty; nobody in Belize City eats catfish, which grow fat with the lazy luxury of their fortunate lives. On the other side of the market is the Court House area. Around Central Park, a small square with grass and hibiscus, are the concrete buildings erected in 1926 by the Jefferson Construction Company that developed Fort George Island. These consist of the Premier's office, the Ministry of Finance and the Treasury, and the imposing Court House, with the Town Clock making a conspicuous ornament. The other sides of the square house Brodie & Company's store on the south, the Royal Bank of Canada on the north, and the commercial buildings on the west, with Barclays Bank and shops. The wooden Court House was originally built in 1818, but was pulled down in 1878; the mahogany posts were found to be in perfect condition after 60 years underground in a tropical climate. Another fine wooden building was put up on a concrete base at a total cost of £5,000. It was painted a creamy white, and had a turret which made it look very like the present Court House. On 17th August, 1918, this building was destroyed in a fire that also brought down the Treasury Building. Governor Hart Bennett was watching the fire and helping to prevent it spreading, when it was noticed that the flagpole had taken fire as well. It was immediately chopped through, and unluckily fell on the governor, who died later of his injuries. On a bronze plaque by the front stairway of the Court House there is a short historical record of the fire. The present buildings, like the bridge over the river, are very strongly built, and have stood up to two hurricanes.

Beyond Central Park are Albert Street and Regent Street, formerly called Back Street and Front Street, both busy thorough-fares of shops and business premises. On Regent Street near the Treasury is the Baron Bliss Institute. That benefactor to British Honduras made a bequest producing $BH40,000 yearly, which has been invested in public buildings and improvements. The Institute contains a theatre and a library, and has a museum of Maya relics. The Library is remarkably well chosen and is well patronized by the people of Belize City who are avid for learn-ing and instruction. In the building are the tragically few books and documents of the history of British Honduras that have escaped the frequent fires and hurricanes, which have destroyed so much of the early records of the Colony.

At the south end of Regent Street is Government House, the Governor's residence, an elegant wooden building of piles, set in a garden from which Hurricane Hattie in 1961 removed most of the trees. Imposing sentries in immaculate uniforms conduct visitors to the Governor's Office overlooking the harbour. This used to be the end of the town in former times, as the edge of the lagoon slopes away to the right sharply, and the land, if land it could be called, was a mass of swamp and mangrove. The Wesleyans built a wall along the south side of the spit and filled in the marsh, and on the land thus reclaimed have built a modern school. A road has been opened to the west along this reclaimed land, and as Belize City is rapidly growing, new houses are filling up the space.

Across the road from Government House is St. John's Cathe-dral Church, built of red brick brought from England, and elegantly finished in Anglican style. The walls inside are covered with plaques, in memory of the people who died of yellow fever in the old days. At times whole shiploads died of the scourge. The last epidemic was in 1905, when the governor's daughter, aged 17, died of the fever and was buried here. The church dates from the year 1812, when the cornerstone was laid by Lieutenant-Colonel John Smyth, then Superintendent of the colony; it was consecrated by the Bishop of Jamaica in 1826, it having taken 14 years in the building. The solid silver font and communion service were donated at the time, and are therefore as old as the church itself. This cathedral has been the scene of three coronations of Mosquito Kings, George Frederick, Robert Charles and George Augustus Frederick. They were crowned there with pomp and ceremony, in the years 1816, 1825 and 1845 respectively. It is on record that the splendours of the coronation of Robert Charles in 1825 cost a thousand pounds.

In addition to the Wesleyan Methodist Church and St. John's Cathedral, there are churches of several other denominations, including Catholics, Baptists and Scottish Presbyterians. In Belize City the Christian has indeed a wide choice of places of worship, both high and low.

Across the lawns of Government House the visitor can see lines of mangroves, and farther out other lines of trees that mark the existence of cays. The Drowned Cays lie two miles away across a tranquil stretch of water, in which there is a tidal rise and fall of no more than two feet. When Hurricane Hattie visited British Honduras, the water of this peaceful lagoon rose 15 feet, and covered the city, raging inland to the airport.

A pleasant promenade runs along the sea wall, with a parapet for people to sit on. Shoals of pipefish swim alongside the wall.

Pelicans and seagulls are common sights in Belize City as are the frigate birds flying high with their long narrow wings and tails. There are not many others. Grackles, like starlings, visit the garden of the hotel, destroying the flowers. In the mouth of the river grampuses snort all day, and little sailing boats ply between Belize City and the outer cays. They come laden with sand and coral rock for the builders, and with cargoes of huge conchs, their shells piling up on the wharf. It is said that the people of Belize are so fond of conchs they eat 2,000 every day. Incredible! Occasionally a raft of logs is towed down from the north; it enters the river to be broken up before going to the sawmills on Haulover Creek.

It is swampy for 10 miles behind Belize City. But along the river banks on terraces coconut cultivation is being attempted. Hurricanes have played havoc with these trees that lie dejected and neglected. Near the airport, where there are some fine willows and mango trees, a high-class hotel has been established for people who like fishing. Being the first of its kind in Belize it has skimmed the cream of the tourist trade. The establishment is exclusive, secluded and expensive. To get there one has to cross the river in a skiff. The hotel is not a luxurious one, consisting of a wooden house with screened veranda, containing the office and dining room, with a small and intimate foyer. Around this are three or four other wooden houses with screened verandas; they contain four bedrooms each. The whole is surrounded by a half-acre garden, with a wooden jetty to the river.

Where the mangroves give way to rushes, there stretches behind Belize City a vast sandy heath dotted with clumps of palmetto scrub, reedy pools, and wild grass. This was once pine forest. Continual logging and forest fires denuded the area. When I crossed this plain in 1962 trunks of pine still smouldered from the forest fire that swept the land after Hurricane Hattie in 1961. Today one has to go 22 miles from Belize City to find the first pine along the western road. After that, trees appear in clumps; regeneration is taking place very slowly. The sandy plain swells gently into long ridges, and here and there the soil in hollows supports a slightly more varied vegetation, but not a soul or a house can be seen for miles. The first mahogany tree appears 39 miles west of Belize City.

About 15 miles inland a small collection of wooden hutments, known as Hattieville, was built as a temporary refuge for those made homeless by the hurricane in 1961.

Fifty miles west of Belize City, at the hub of the major north-south and east-west highways, 55 miles from Stann Creek Town, and 30 miles from the Guatemalan border, is the site of the new capital. Formal approval of the project was given in 1962, after which feasibility studies, soil, water and drainage tests were carried out. In October 1965, Mr. Anthony Greenwood, then Secretary of State for the Colonies, unveiled a commemorative stele at the site. It takes the form of a stone pillar with a plaque, and for over a year stood forlorn, like a Maya pyramid in the forest. A new pyramid will go up to house the Legislative Assembly. Its design is modernistic, with a touch of ancient Maya temple. It will be constructed on the highest point to command a view of the other Government offices in the new city.

The project will be financed at a cost of over $BH20,000,000, of which the British Government has undertaken to provide a contribution of $BH16,500,000 in grants and loans for the first phase, which by 1970 is calculated to have a nucleus population of 5,000 people. Plans include banks, hotels, offices, churches, schools and private houses, well equipped with pure piped water, sewage disposal, diesel generated electric power and a VHF radio-telephone link.

Work on the new capital is now in full swing. Seventy-six duplex houses were built to provide accommodation for the contractors and their workmen, and in the first phase 740 houses of five basic types will be established. By 1970 the new capital will be a living community.

The port of Stann Creek Town lies 35 miles south of Belize City, but by road one has to travel 105 miles along three sides of an irregular quadrangle of impenetrable swamp. The Western Highway, for the first 50 miles crosses the sandy heath, until by the new capital site, it turns south into the foothills of the Maya Mountains. The soil here is more productive, and although pines predominate there is an increasing variety of trees festooned with creepers, the convolvulus flowers growing purple, blue and white. This is 'low bush', logged out, its natural vegetation slowly recovering from the frequent fires. It is not entirely uninhabited; occasional shanties are to be seen in clearings, but the population is sparse. The Creoles there eke out a living with the help of shotguns. They never stir along the road without a gun on their shoulder, for any creature that walks or crawls is food. They tell hair-raising tales of jaguars, eight feet long, weighing 400 pounds. But during the day one sees no animals along the road and very few birds, except white egrets and an occasional turkey buzzard wheeling in the sky. In the darkness nightjars, called 'whoyous', flutter in front of the car lights. There is a superstition in British Honduras that these birds' eggs, laid in nests in low bushes, can never be burnt: a bush will burn down without affecting the eggs. Perhaps the 'whoyou' makes a nest of green twigs wich refuse to flare up. At night opossums wander too leisurely for their own good, for their crushed bodies are strewn along the highway.

The unpaved road is not bad, but unexpected potholes form along its gravelled surface. The car bumps along for another 25 miles until it enters a district where the soil is deeper and blacker, and the citrus plantations begin. The land is broken into deep, narrow valleys – a state of geologic youth; here is another reminder that in a recent epoch all British Honduras had been raised from the sea. The sandy heath behind Belize City was until recently a wide bay.

Names are picturesque but not accurate; near the site of the new capital is the little village of Roaring Creek. The stream itself is a placid little thing, which does not even babble over the stones. Farther along the road crosses Hell's Teeth Creek, which might be Roaring Creek's little brother, so mild is the watercourse. The colony is full of remarkable names: Coqueri-cot, which is the Spanish version of Cockadoodle-do, Double Head Cabbage, Bread and Butter Cay, Wee-wee Cay (this last named for the wee-wee or parasol leaf-cutting ant), More-Force, Bound-to-Shine and More Tomorrow. The origin of these names is never satisfactorily explained.

Take the name Stann Creek, for example. On the map of 1786, which is the earliest available, the name is Stand Creek. This name is derived, according to some authorities, from the word 'Stand', which used to mean an open roadstead anchorage for ships. Other authorities say the 'Stand', meant a warehouse of goods at the site. But where else in the English-speaking world is the word used in either sense?

Stann Creek Town, is a pleasant little place, inhabited by Creoles and Caribs and a few Chinese who have shops. The little river that gives it its name runs placidly through the town to a beautiful beach of smooth sand, stretching for miles along the shore. The jetty from which oranges, grapefruit and orange juice concentrate are shipped to Canada and the United Kingdom is at Commerce Bight, two miles south of Stann Creek. The place was razed by the hurricane in 1961, and has been largely rebuilt, partly out of the remains of the former wooden buildings, partly with new wood and the self-help loan programme of the government. The Mayor's office and the public administration buildings are in concrete blocks, and are Stann Creek Town's pride. Loans from Great Britain have provided a new power plant, with a diesel generating set, and the power runs a public water supply from wells, ample for the needs of Stann Creek Town.

We went to Georgetown and Silk Grass, two little settlements for hurricane refugees, who were transferred out of Stann Creek Town and encouraged to start smallholdings on unoccupied land. Each settlement is a collection of wooden cottages of two rooms each; in British Honduras one will find in the smallest village a school and a recreational centre. We went through Silk Grass, waving to the policeman-telegraphist, and stopped in Georgetown. We had to stop before long, for the road was a quagmire, and not even a Land-Rover would have made the trip. The people were Caribs. They speak little English, although they can if they have to. Little children came to gaze at the spectacle – it is not every day that strangers come to town. They were not in the least shy nor ill-mannered.

The chairman of the village council came to say good-day. He was an elderly Carib, who left his garden, hoe in hand, a veritable Cincinnatus, with the natural charm and simple dignity of these people.

The countryside was low bush and palmetto heath, with soil very sandy in places; it changed to clay towards the interior. We took a new road, opened up by graders only a short time ago. It was wide and smooth, but soft in places. We arrived at a small culvert, which had carried a trickle under the road. Rain the night before had enlarged the stream and filled the culvert with sand, so the brook had had to make a new bed – across the roadway. There was a bay of water about 20 yards wide. It was only a few inches deep but deceptive. In trying to circumnavigate the pool we stuck in the mud. We made mats of pine branches and reeds from the heath, and managed to move the car a yard farther before it stuck even deeper. I thought of night and jaguars, and decided that I would raise the window of the car on my side.

With all the drama of an adventure film we were rescued by the British Army. We had not been half an hour in the mud when we heard a lorry coming round the bend in the road from Stann Creek Town. It turned out to be the first of a caravan of Army vehicles, the Staffordshire Regiment out on exercise. Beefy lads were lolling back in troop carriers, wearing hats like amateur gardeners' or driving Land-Rovers hitched to mysterious pieces of artillery. They tore through the puddle, and proved that it was only six inches deep and had a firm bottom. Someone shouted:

'Major's in the last jeep but four, and last vehicle is Recovery. They'll pull you out; we can't stop'.

How to tell which was the last vehicle but four when one

could not see the end of the line? But an officer did stop to supervise our rescue by Recovery, which turned out to be an enormous lorry, with an unfortunate recruit who had to get his feet wet tying the cable on to our car. We came out with a bow-wave like a motor launch, unscathed, and continued our journey to Independence. The angels had been on our side; there was not a human being within 15 miles, and we could have been stranded all night.

At Independence, in 1962, the Hercules Powder Company of Delaware, USA, installed a large plant to extract resin from the pine stumps left after logging in the region. It was expected that enough raw material was available to last at least 10 years; the cost of the installation at $US5,000,000 was not excessive for the results to be obtained. However, in less than three years the plant closed down, and was removed to Nicaragua. Two hundred families of workers were left without employment, which created a serious economic problem, and their redeployment created a social problem. Some of the men could be placed in the new sugar refinery in the Corozal district, but that was over 100 miles from Independence by road, and the transfer of the families inevitably meant in many cases the separation of husbands from wives and parents from children.

The discharged workers were not the only people to suffer, for a number of businesses had grown up around the plant – shops and recreational facilities, which were indirectly dependent on the plant and the salaries it paid out. Surveying the silent empty wooden hutments that had housed the operatives, nobody could understand why the plant closed down so soon.

The official reason given was that the price of resins in the United States of America had fallen to a point at which it was no longer profitable to run the factory; but it was generally held that an error had been made in the calculation of the number of stumps available.

At the time resentment in British Honduras was felt towards the company, and it was severely criticized for what was held to be unfeeling indifference to any consideration other than profits. The prospect of a large investment and increased employment at higher wages had created an illusion of prosperity, which made the disappointment and distress felt all the more keenly. Perhaps the venture provided the internal government of British Honduras, then cautiously feeling its way in sociology, with a good example of what to avoid – the impact of major financial operations on a small impecunious community can often be more disastrous than beneficial.

About 60 miles south of Independence is the little seaside town of Punta Gorda (Broad Point in Spanish), the last sizeable place before arriving at the frontier with Guatemala. A charming resort, inhabited by Caribs, it is the administrative centre of the district which produces rice and beans, which are boiled together and with meat balls comprise the national dish of British Honduras. The place boasts a good modern hospital of 35 beds, under the charge of a competent physician, with three German nuns as his assistants. The houses are of wood, and although the little jetty can be crowded with the boats of the coastal trade, it is not a real seaport. As a centre of tourism it could be unsurpassed. The reef and cays in front and the Indian villages of the hinterland remain unspoilt. Formerly it was impossible to get there except by sea; but roads are being opened and maintained all over the south of British Honduras. By air-taxi to Belize City would take an hour or less. It would be comfortable, but I would prefer to go by boat and enjoy the company of the people of Belize, and I would ask them to sing Carib songs, like 'Chila my sister'.

On the Western highway towards Benque Viejo del Carmen is San Ignacio, the centre of the Cayo district. The only other places larger than a village are Orange Walk Town and Corozal Town in the northern part of the colony. Corozal was destroyed completely by Hurricane Janet in 1955, and lost its distinctive semi-Mexican style of adobe walls, called 'marl' in British Honduras. It was entirely rebuilt with much public aid. The site of the old hospital is now a public park, and the new hospital is a modern building at the edge of the town. The houses have been made partly of wood, some on stilts, like Belize City or Stann Creek Town. Corozal flourishes because of the presence of the big sugar refinery of Tate & Lyle, Ltd. at Libertad, about eight miles south of the town. Corozal is the first place in British Honduras on the way down from Mexico, crossing over the Rio Hondo, the Deep River, by a large and modern suspension bridge, which the government of Mexico built in 1964. There is no town at the frontier; Chetumal in the State of Quintana

Roo is several miles farther on – a favourite place for excursions from Belize. Formalities at the frontier are at a minimum; but Chetumal is not British Honduras and I did not go there.

A 'Sah mamma' – descendant of one of the old Belizeans who came from Jamaica.

6. CREOLES, CARIBS AND OTHER PEOPLE

THE Premier of British Honduras, the Honourable George Price, accorded me an interview. He was most co-operative. He wished me well, and passed on a few ideas of his own: 'Please,' he said, 'do not stress the differences between our people. Instead, emphasize the common identity of the people living in British Honduras. Do not say Creole, or Carib, or Mestizo. Use the expressions Afro-Belizean, Carib-Belizean or Maya-Belizean. Or better still, use only the word Belizean.'

The Premier has based his policy on building up a new nation in Central America to be called Belize, and from his political mountain top he is very right. The most important factor in public life in the Colony today is the determination to form a new nation. Ultimately a homogeneous population will evolve from the various elements of today. That end has yet to be achieved. If, therefore, we use the names Creole and Carib, without tacking on the political tailpiece of 'Belizean', it is not from a desire to disregard the aspirations of the Premier. Rather do we note the diversity of race in order to bring out still more clearly the unity of purpose; for the diversity of human types in British Honduras is most remarkable.

On the streets of Belize City one can meet practically every shade of pigmentation, and the mixing continues. In a hundred years none of the extremes will exist because of interbreeding by marriage and through casual unions.

The original white inhabitant was a Scot whose ghost still pervades the Creole dialect which is the common medium of communication. The Baymen as a class have long since been extinct. Their descendants, who may still use the Scottish surnames so common in Belize City, have been absorbed in the Creole population. Most of those white men must have had African women as their house servants and as their concubines. Families of British origin exist today in Belize City, but they have been recent immigrants. One intelligent and observant person ventured the assertion that there were no pure-blooded inhabitants of any race now left, with the exception of late arrivals, such as the Lebanese. There are already young people of half Syrian blood, products of intermarriage with mestizo or Creole. The use of the surname alone can reveal the nationality of the ancestor, and in many families the most varied pattern of skin colour prevails, and features vary among brothers and sisters.

If the original Baymen had formed a senatorial body like the patricians of Rome, they might have survived as a social class; but the lumber trade converged into the hands of a large corporation of overseas ownership, with absentee landlords.

Having to wait in the building of the Royal Bank of Canada in Belize while the manager attended to more useful members of the community, I used my time to take a census of the clients whom I surmised to be a cross-section of middle class Belize City. Of 54 persons who passed through the swing door I counted 30 whom I would call, in my superficial and inexperienced way, negroes. I disregarded facial types, as I had no time nor ability to remember the cross classification. Therefore, of the people of the capital city, over 55 per cent I supposed were Afro-Belizeans, and under 45 per cent must be mulattoes, mestizos and intermediate types.

I took the matter to the Information Office. 'What,' I said bravely, 'is a Creole really? Does it mean a person of African descent?'

Not necessarily predominantly African descent, they said, but certainly partially. All the people who entered the bank in that half hour had been Creoles. The word, originally French, meant a Frenchman born in the West Indian colonies. Similarly, in Spanish the word 'criollo' signified a person of pure Spanish lineage, born in America. In British Honduras the word had a different meaning; it meant a person with some African blood, mixed in varying degree. Some very dark men have European features. The long forearm and lower leg of the typical negro are common in the Colony; this makes many of the men exceptionally tall – lanky fellows, rather slender for their height. But they can be hefty and broad, and then they are really big men; the police force of Belize City and the British Honduras Volunteer Guard are noted for their fine appearance. Destiny chose for their forefathers the pick of West Africa, men of strength and en-

ight : Sir William (later Admiral) Burnaby. ı 1765 he arrived at Belize from Jamaica to ve protection against the Spaniards. He ganized the loggers, or Baymen, politically, ving them a 'Code' – 'The Ancient Usages ıd Customs of the Settlement'.

elow : A model of the central area of the ew Capital Site. This city-to-be, about ɔo feet above sea level, is almost in the ntre of the country. The site for this long-ınge project was opened in October 1965 y Mr. Anthony Greenwood, then Secretary ̆ State for the Colonies.

Aerial view of Belize City, the capital of British Honduras. *Below left:* A corner of Central Park, Belize City. *Below right:* Site of the new capital, which, by 1970, will house about 5,000 people. The new capital will relieve congestion in Belize City and also help in the development of the surrounding villages.

Fresh fruit arriving by sailboat at Mango Creek. The Belize Estate saw mill is here; most of the lumber sawn comes from a large stand of pine nearby. *Below:* A view of Commerce Street in Stann Creek, one of the five administrative districts into which the country is divided.

The new Tower Hill bridge spanning the New River in the Orange Walk District. It is the last link in an uninterrupted road from Belize City to the neighbouring country to the north, Mexico. *Below :* The Tate and Lyle sugar factory. The production and export of sugar is one of the most important industries in British Honduras.

Below : Spanish Indian worker on a plantation, Corozal District. The cane here and in Orange Walk District has a very high sucrose content.

Hauling timber – mahogany – at Mountain Pine Ridge, Cayo District. The famous mahogany of British Honduras is now almost exhausted.

A herdsman with Red Poll cattle in the Cayo District. The alluvial soil here yields excellent forage for cattle grazing.

In the Waha Leaf banana plantation Mango Creek area. An average of 200,000 stems of bananas are exported annually

Citrus groves at Pomona in the Stann Creek District. The industry processes frozen orange juice concentrate and makes canned orange juice and grapefruit segments. Many groves of oranges and grapefruit are owned by the processers.

In the machine workshop of the Belize Technical College, which is making a valuable contribution to the supply of skilled manpower in British Honduras.

Sixth-form students of biology at the St. John's College, a Jesuit institution. It has a new industrial arts section and the first batch of graduates recently received their diplomas.

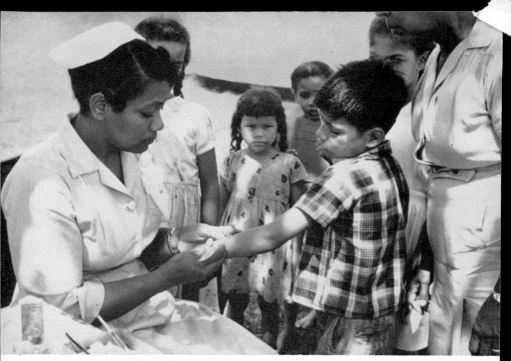

BCG vaccinations at Burrel Boom. Such personal health services are being steadily expanded. *Below:* Examining pottery fragments from the Maya ruins at Rockstone Park. A field team carrying out excavations is being directed by Dr. D. M. Prendergast, Professor of Anthropology, University of Utah, USA.

durance. Their women can be tall, too; and when they are broad, they can reach enormous size – up to 18 or 20 stone. Yet little women, slender and graceful, abound in Belize City. Their fingers are long and artistic, dark on top and pink underneath, and they have eyes like fawns.

In former times the scourge of the Colony was yellow fever, but this disease has been completely eliminated by modern medical and sanitary science, and it is over 50 years since any cases were reported in British Honduras. In our generation malaria has almost disappeared but a few cases occur every year. The statistics of hospital cases and bills of mortality show no conspicuous difference from any other modern well-conducted town.

British Hondurans are usually healthy. Hospital records show no tendency to a particular tropical disease. It is most remarkable that dysentery in children, green diarrhoea that carries off thousands of infants in tropical America, is less frequent in Belize than it is in Great Britain. The high standard of personal hygiene may have something to do with this, for the Creoles are noticeably good ablutioners. African races are said to have better teeth than Europeans, but that is not the case in British Honduras, where a good set is the exception. The incidence of venereal disease is half that of the other Central American countries. Among police recruits and applicants for nursing training who have Wasserman tests on examination, about ten per cent will show a positive reaction, which must indicate congenital as well as acquired infection.

I decided in Belize to try to get solicited. The most strategic post for the experiment would be the middle of the bridge over the Haulover Creek, and there I stationed myself at eight o'clock one evening. All Belize City seemed to be rushing by, but no dusky maidens approached. Instead, a very large policeman loomed up. He was about 30 years younger than I, and at least a foot taller. Whatever he said would prevail over my intention.

'Sir,' said this guardian of Her Majesty's peace and order, 'do you not perceive that there are regulations for the circulation in transit?' I circulated in transit back to the hotel.

When I told people of my attempt they gave me the very surprising piece of news that no organized prostitution exists in British Honduras. That is probably true; but it does not mean that no prostitution of any kind takes place. Naughty girls in tight red pants will beckon from doorways, as I found out later in my entirely innocent strolls through the streets of Belize City.

The temperament of Creoles in British Honduras is placid and good humoured. 'We laugh at each other and go on to the next joke,' they explained to me. If one were called upon to give in one word their main characteristic, one could reply: 'Kindliness'.

'Tell me,' I asked a Creole friend, 'what is the word in Creole for a white person?'

He was embarrassed.

'Come now,' I protested at his silence, 'there must be some word for a European. If you call yourselves Creoles, you must have the complementary term for people who are not Creoles.'

'Well,' he replied with diffidence, 'in Creole we say *bakra* for a white person.'

'And what is the derivation of the term? Is it a word brought over from Africa?'

'Why, no,' he said smiling at last. 'It is English. It comes from *back raw*, because white people blister their backs and peel after they take off their shirts in the sun.'

Having observed some lady tourists who had gone out fishing in short pants, I could appreciate how graphic the word was. He went on quickly:

'Please don't think it is contemptuous. Rather is it expressive of pity for people who cannot enjoy the pleasant warmth of the sun for as long as ourselves.'

On the sea front by the Memorial Park a fisherman sat in a canoe made from a hollowed-out tree-trunk. He paddled to a post set in the water about 20 yards from the shore. To this he tied a stout line; he threw into the water a large hook attached to a short piece of chain and as bait he had a yellowish fish the size of a herring. Then he paddled back to the wall and sat. The line drifted slowly out with the tidal stream. I sat down beside him and asked:

'Is that a good way to fish here?'

'Sir,' he replied in perfect English, 'it is the best at this time. At other times of the moon I can go out, and in a couple of hours

I come back with the boat full of fish. Now perhaps I catch a jewfish as big as myself.'

He was not the usual lanky Belizean. Nature had equipped him with the head and body of a normal man, but had short-changed him in the matter of limbs, for he was of the dachshund build, with arms and legs half the usual length.

'Then,' I observed, 'you must make a good thing of it, selling that fish in the market of Belize.'

He looked at me, astonished. Then it dawned on him that he was dealing with an ignoramus.

'Sir, you do not understand,' he explained gently. 'In Belize City nobody sells fish. Everyone gives to everyone else.'

It is true that the implementation here of a modern system of paying tribute presents some difficulties to economic planners. The Belizean method, however, has its merits in preparation for the Day of Resurrection.

Of course they do sell fish in Belize City. What the fishermen was trying to express was his emotional generosity, not the economic situation of the fish trade in British Honduras. There is a fish market in Belize City and flourishing fish markets in the other coastal towns.

Creoles speak their own language among themselves. It grades imperceptibly into English. Spoken in its rich fullness it is as different a language as Danish or German. To give only two examples: 'Chew gwine' means 'Are you going', and seems to be derived from the negative interrogative, 'Aren't you going?' although it is used as an affirmative. 'Cungo dey' means 'Let us go there'. To hear the real language, not a semi-English dialect, a visitor should creep across Central Park to the cement bench on which sit the waiting taxidrivers. Before they spot his presence and change into business English, the eavesdropper will have heard real Creole. The pronunciation has a richness that no European alphabet can reproduce, and is best enunciated in shouts. The most effective way would be to hold a conversation with a friend across the main street of the City with up-roarious jokes.

We stood on the sea wall and watched a man in a boat below. He was obviously going out fishing, with a tangle of lines, a tin-can of bait and what seemed to be several cans of Dutch beer, in case of shipwreck. The boat had one of those outboard motors with a whirligig on top, round which the expeditionist wound a lanyard and tugged. The motor said 'Muckapick' and was silent. He re-wound the cord and tugged afresh. The engine went 'Muckapick, muckapick' and was silent again.

Tension among the onlookers grew intolerable. One leant forward and enquired in English, no doubt for the benefit of the *bakra* present:

'Man, can you not manipulate the mechanism?'

The fellow in the boat looked up and opened his mouth very wide, showing that he had no upper front teeth and no lower back ones. He shouted, 'Wahoo wahee', or words to that effect in Creole. The other shouted back, abandoning English for a more ample vocabulary in Creole. It seemed to be technical instruction about outboard motors. The man in the boat twiddled a few knobs, and then restrung his whirligig, and gave it a real long pull. The motor roared; he sat down, waved his hand to the cheering crowd, and chugged out to the cays.

All Creoles speak English and Creole, and a considerable number speak Central American Spanish, which differs from the Castillian and South American forms in minor points. Their English at times tends to be very stately, but they do not use exaggerated metaphors or clichés. The Creoles of Belize City, who use their long words somewhat quaintly, choose them with care and try to express themselves with logic and clarity. They never use blasphemous or obscene phrases. Since swearwords only have use for relaxing tension, and Creoles seem to be eternally relaxed, they have no need for expletives.

It has been said, and too frequently, that Creoles do not like work. However, when we say a man is energetic and dynamic, we usually mean he is scrambling to accumulate material goods. The Creoles of British Honduras are not interested in getting rich; they consider this unnatural.

A well-meaning tourist in the hotel lobby said to a taxi driver: 'We did not see you around last night and so we had to get another chauffeur. Didn't you want to make a dollar?'

'Sir,' replied the taximan, 'Last night I did not make money. I made love.'

He probably got a better return for his outlay of energy. When the people of British Honduras want to work at something which they value more than money, they can labour mightily. They are building up their country, and that is worth hard work, and their efforts are not without results already.

Living side by side with the Creole is the Carib. He is darker than the Creole, for he has no white blood. The Caribs are the descendants of Arawak Indians from the Orinoco who interbred with negroes. They were a terror to sugar planters for two centuries, and many armed expeditions were sent against them. They lived in the island of St. Vincent until about the beginning of the nineteenth century, when they began to settle in Central America; they are to be found in small numbers along the east coast of Spanish Honduras and Nicaragua. In 1797 they were on Roatán in the islands of the Bay of Honduras and in 1823 they asked for permission to settle in the south of British Honduras. This was accorded them. They now number some 10,000, mostly in the Stann Creek district.

One can easily confuse a Creole with a Carib. The Carib shows his Indian descent in his broader face and low, wide forehead, whereas the Creole has a narrow head with its frontal bosses. They share the good nature and generosity of the Creole, and speak their own language. It is perhaps derived from Africa with some additions and borrowings from English, Spanish and French. Creoles do not speak Carib, but Caribs speak Creole, and most of them will speak good English and Spanish as well. They travel much between British Honduras and the coasts of Guatemala, Honduras and the isles of the bay, and have relatives living in those parts. Generally, they adopted Spanish surnames – Moreira, Zúniga, and the like; and use English Christian names.

The Caribs have a remarkable aptitude for study and a capacity for learning. The schoolmasters of British Honduras are largely Caribs, teaching in Maya, Carib, Creole and English. On one of my trips I had as an interpreter in the Maya villages, Mr. Faustino John Zúniga, whose facility in English, Spanish, Creole, Carib, Kekchi and Mopán Maya was astounding. He rang the changes from one language to another without a hitch or fumble.

The Caribs have a rich folklore of songs, which is being recorded in writing and on magnetic tapes. The government of the Colony is particularly anxious not to lose this treasure of culture. Their music is simple and sentimental. There is a splendid opportunity for a person technically trained to make a study of their music and literature. New compositions in Carib are coming forward, and are as popular in Stann Creek Town and Punta Gorda as anything from the theatres in London and New York.

In Punta Gorda we called on Miss Venancia Petrillo, a lady known to all as Miss Ben. My escort and sponsor was Mr. Ronald Clark, of the Information Office. The Premier, Mr. Price, had eaten in her house the day before and we had supper there. It was beef stew with potatoes and cabbage and her own home-made bread, washed down with large cups of tea.

'Miss Ben,' announced Mr. Clark with due solemnity, 'there is going to be a Music Festival in Belize City in May, and a prize for the best chorus singing Carib songs. Now I know your group of ladies is very enthusiastic, but I warn you Stann Creek Town is sending a very strong team.'

Miss Ben heads a folklore society in Punta Gorda, and her singing ladies are first rate. Mr. Clark began to sing 'Chila my sister' in Carib, and Miss Ben joined in, while I listened entranced.

Next morning we breakfasted on fried eggs and fried beans and more home-made bread. I was duly primed by Mr. Zúniga and piped up on arrival:

'Buite binahe, Miss Ben'. Good morning, in Carib.

'Buite binahe', she responded and then came the delayed reflex: 'Why, he learn Carib already! Wait! I join you at breakfast.'

She came in and drank a cup of tea while we stuffed ourselves; I noticed she did not eat anything. Probably she had breakfasted long before we arrived. When we were going we gave thanks in Carib:

'Tanke ñeabu, Miss Ben.'

In Miss Ben's house in Punta Gorda I tried some cassava bread. It was hard tack biscuit made of the starch from the cassava root, and tastes like hard starch. It needs a lot of chewing to go down willingly, but could replace rice and beans, or potatoes, or wheat bread as a base in a diet; but I would call it an acquired taste.

Another more recent immigrant community is formed by the Mennonites, who first came to British Honduras about 20 years ago.

The Mennonite sect derives its name from a preacher in Germany, Menno Simons, who was himself a Dutchman, born in 1492; he died in 1559. When the Reformation broke out, some German peasants took the Bible as their guide in life and interpreted that teaching in a very literal sense. As Christians they studied the New Testament and came to the conclusion that a true believer would not carry arms, hold political office, swear oaths or resort to the law courts. They revived in the Europe of the Middle Ages the civil disobedience that the earliest Christians had practised against Rome. Naturally they ran counter not only to the Catholic ecclesiastical hierarchy's authority, but also to any authority that replaced it in any country. Isolation was the only alternative to extinction or absorption; thus isolation has been the salient feature of the Mennonite life to this day. Supremely introverted, they shrank from contact with the sinful world around them, and crystallized their way of life. It remains unchanged – a piece of sixteenth century German peasantry, a social fossil in the twentieth.

Mennonites were organized in Germany from the remnants of the Anabaptist movement after the persecutions in the Peasants' War. Although Menno Simons was not the originator of the movement, it was his name they took to distinguish themselves from the rest of the world. Some settled in Russia in the eighteenth century, speaking a dialect of German that was archaic even then. In the next 100 years they incurred the disapproval of the Russian authorities, as they opposed the conscription of their youth into the Czarist armies. They were therefore driven out of Russia and some settled in America. There are Mennonite colonies in the United States and Canada, and from one of the Canadian settlements are derived the Mennonites of British Honduras. At first they had sought freedom of action in the north; but the insistence of the Canadian government that they send their children to public schools provoked stubborn disobedience. They therefore went to Chihuahua in Mexico, where they purchased land and devoted themselves to the farming that is the only occupation for the true Mennonite. In Mexico, however, they suffered the same 'persecution' that they had experienced in Canada – they were told that their children must go to public schools and learn to be good Mexican citizens; they refused. They were prosecuted and called it persecution. They sought a further home which they found in British Honduras.

After the second world war Mennonites purchased a tract of

land in the centre of British Honduras and started to build up their own world. Very successfully they did so too, unmolested and unharried by such things as other people's laws, but very well aware that the British Crown gave them a security that they had never known before. Their energy and agricultural knowledge soon converted the low bush into fertile fields, and also reduced by half the cost of chickens and eggs in the country.

According to the last census there were 2,811 Mennonites in the Colony, consisting of 444 families. There are four communities: at Spanish Lookout in the centre of the country, about 70 miles west of Belize City, the biggest and most liberal in outlook, and at Bluecreek, Shipyard and Richmond Hill in the Orange Walk district, more to the north. These last three are stricter and more isolated from the rest of society. They really are self-perpetuating monastic communities, in which celibacy is not practised.

The Mennonite communities are legal corporations. They own the land which they purchased outright in 1957 for an average price of $BH3.00 or 15 shillings an acre. It would cost them $10 or $12 now. They hold 148,500 acres, of which they cultivate only 12,010 acres as yet; they therefore have plenty of space to expand without impinging on other people's lives. Spanish Lookout sends its agricultural produce to a Mennonite Centre in Belize City. which acts as marketing board under the management of Mr. Paul Martin, a member of a Mennonite community from Lancaster, in Pennsylvania, USA. The Centre handles 200 crates of eggs weekly and half a ton of tomatoes.

The settlement at Spanish Lookout resembles at first glance those photographs of the Ohio and Mississippi backwoods of the last century. The fields are full of stumps awaiting removal by haulage or decay; at the back of the fields the looming forest closes in. The houses are vaguely reminiscent of Pennsylvanian barns, well built of boards and painted white. The inhabitants are German farm labourers, fair-haired, well-built lads, speaking a home-made German patois, and the girls are frauleins with pigtails. They receive no education past primary school, and then go to work on the farms, which are fairly widely separated from each other. The most striking difference between these communities and the usual British Honduras village is the way in which they receive a visitor from the outside world. Shock haired children peer at one from doorways, and matrons discreetly peep behind curtains. This amounts almost to indifference when compared with the crowded reception one gets in a Creole or Carib community. Mennonites return a greeting from a stranger; but it was noticeable that they are never the first to give it.

The population of British Honduras doubles itself every 25 years, and in a century hence it may well reach the million mark. The communities of Mennonites will have increased too. Will they mingle socially and politically, or will they remain as they are, a state within the State?

There is no racial problem in British Honduras; no striving for white or black supremacy or equality; for social barriers do not exist. It is very probable that they never have existed in the Colony. John Stevens, the American writer who visited Central America in the 1840s, and wrote a book about his travels, came to Belize and attended the court there while a civil case was being heard. He noted the equality between the black and white elements in the place, even so soon after the abolition of slavery. Today the pure white element in the population is so small in number that it can claim no pre-eminence in any direction.

Carib woman collecting water at Stann Creek.
In the background are typical houses on stilts.

F

The popular Carib song:

'CHILA MY SISTER'

Chila niturou wou innihan sandi aduga bullah nou
Chila niturou wou innihan sandi aduga bullah nou
Aibuga nallai louba indura mah
Alluga arani, darraya arani.

Nouweya san igira nayame namulenu narriguen
Nouweya san igira nayame namulenu narriguen
Nidiba aguyo houn libanyan baba
Ariha namugana lubara nouwey.

Bayahuwaha lege nagamba luagu bugundan lan
Bayahuwaha lege nagamba luagu bugundan lan
Ragabai baguira nitu araida bai
Innitegua weyo luni bayahuahan

'CHILA MY SISTER'
(English translation)

Chila, my sister, illness is poking fun at me;
Chila, my sister, illness is poking fun at me.
I have walked Honduras in search of medicine –
The medicine is finished.

Am I going to die and leave the grandchildren
　of my parents behind?
Am I going to die and leave the grandchildren
　of my parents behind?
I will go home to my folks,
So I may see them before I die.

You cry and then I learned that you take pleasure
　in doing so,
You cry and then I learned that you take pleasure
　in doing so.
Wipe your tears and save them –
The day will come when you'll have need of them.

7. MAYAS, DEAD AND ALIVE

OF Maya Indians in British Honduras there are two groups, the live and the dead, the latter being of absorbing interest to some people. It is not to be denied that they left their footprints very impressively all over the country; but their descendants in the flesh are preferable.

About the time that the Pharaohs of Egypt were building their pyramids, Maya Indians began to cultivate maize. Where they found the plant cannot be ascertained now; but it is reasonable to suppose that it grew on the slopes of the Central American Cordillera. It provided a staple diet that afforded them enough leisure to develop a Neolithic culture. At the primitive levels of 'milpa' cultivation, maize requires only three months labour a year: for felling the bush, burning the trash at the end of the dry season, planting after the first rains have fallen in May, doubling over the stalks when the cob ripens (so that the grains do not get wet and start sprouting) and weeding the beans and pumpkins planted between the stalks. That was the Indians' yearly round; today it is largely the same.

Naturally, the nine months of leisure were well used by the organisers of Maya society. Labour was controlled by the state authorities. They required a calendar to calculate the arrival of the rainy season and, no doubt, to forecast lucky and unlucky dates. Their 'cities' in the forests, whose ruins so captivate archaeologists, professional and amateur, were probably in the first place solar observatories. From their observations and a system of numeration that included zero signs, they formed a calendar; which worked well enough for them and by enthusiasts is said to be more accurate than ours. They had no metals during all their history, except some imported gold in later years. However, the soft limestone of Central America, which hardens on exposure to the weather, is an admirable material for construction, easily extracted and easily carved with stone chisels. Whenever they finished some notable stage of pyramid or temple, they erected a four-square pillar, which archaeologists call a 'stele', and obligingly carved the date on the back.

Thus we know that there were three stages of Maya development before the culture collapsed after A D 1000. The first was in the millenium before Christ; the second was in the first years of our era; the last, before the collapse and submergence of the civilization, was about the time of William the Conqueror. The first Maya cities in British Honduras, now being scientifically excavated, had been erected coevally with the Anglo-Saxon heptarchy, and flourished at the time of Alfred the Great.

When the Maya civilization was at its height it is calculated that the population of British Honduras was about 750,000. This was not a separate political state. The general Maya Empire in Guatemala, Honduras and southern Mexico comprised a population of about 15,000,000, far more than the area supports today. Where now we see only the waving tops of trees there was then a largely cleared countryside of brown patches of cultivation alternating with green fallow. Roads connected each 'city' with the others. When the limestone pyramids and temples were new and white, with deeply cut carvings along the friezes and cornices, the centres of culture must have been very handsome. There were no wheeled carts, but sledges must have been in use to move the limestone blocks; hosts of porters would have been running at a trot, as Indians still do today under heavy loads, transporting goods slung from the forehead by a band.

It is conventional to praise the ancient Maya civilization as a thing beyond compare, whose disappearance has been an irretrievable loss to humanity. In reality, they were less advanced than the Egyptians or the Sumerians of the Neolithic age. They had no domestic animals, except perhaps the dog and the turkey while the Incas of South America had already domesticated the llama. The usual architecture was limited to a roof of palm frond thatch, with or without walls of canes. The massive stone pyramids were public works, and even those consisted of mere heaps of stones. If they resemble the pyramids of Egypt that is only because all primitive cultures will heap up similar mounds. There is no detail of the Maya civilization that points to recent affinity with any other.

However, even though their grasp of mechanical arts may have been limited, there must have been a high degree of co-operation among the members of the community to raise those piles. The rulers must have been despotic men, with absolute control over the spare time of the common citizen; but at some period in the development of the Maya race this obedience ceased. The labour for the maintenance of public works became scarcer. Finally all repair work was abandoned and no new monuments were erected. Guessing the reason for this failure of social organization is a favourite pastime for archaeologists in Central America. After 1,500 years of success the Mayan way of life became unpopular, and finally was rejected by the same men who had invented it.

The collapse was not as sudden as it seems at a distance of several centuries. There was no foreign invasion which overthrew a god-descended dynasty and the expounders of the one true faith. The prince and the bishop were compounded under one authority, although the priest and the warrior apparently were not identical. Some diggers-up of ancient Maya tombs claim that there are traces of desecration still visible, and deduce therefrom a religious reformation, or rejection of the national and time-honoured deities and their servants, the priests and wise men. Others think that an increase of population so reduced the amount of fallow that the necessary recuperation periods were shortened to the point of crop failure, or at least crop reduction to a near famine level. This might cause a mass emigration to better and richer soil; and, indeed, some Maya centres were abandoned while others were blooming, showing that artisans and rulers emigrated together. It was a slow drift from south to north, from Spanish Honduras to Mexico, and not until they were in decadence did the Mayas come in contact with foreign nations. First they met the Olmecs, then the Toltecs, and then the Aztecs; and behind the Aztecs, were the Chichimecs, relatives of the Comanches and the Shoeshones far to the north.

Whatever might have been the cause, the Mayas grew bored with their expensive civilization and its overbearing optimates, and allowed the great plazas to become choked with weeds. Trees sprouted on the sloping sides of the pyramids, until the tropical forest swallowed up the sites, whose very names were forgotten. The Mayas were not completely submerged when the Spaniards came to America. The sundry nations in what is now Guatemala were in a fairly prosperous and cohesive state. The Mayas in that republic still speak their ancient dialects, and observe some of their ancient customs and beliefs. They have absorbed, however, much of the Spanish way of life. New vegetables and new utensils made them adopt Spanish words for they had no native terms, for instance, for the onion or the mirror.

In the Yucatán peninsula the Mayas were virtually untouched until a campaign in 1691 reduced them to nominal subjection to the Spanish monarchy. In practice nothing was done except to establish a few churches; the emotional content of the Christian religion was found to be acceptable by the Mayas, who largely adopted that faith. Their real conquest and forced inclusion into the proletariat of our modern world lasted from 1848 until 1880. When the Spanish monarchy went the way of the ancient Maya priesthood-aristocracy, the Mexican republic failed to fill the political vacuum in the Peninsula of Yucatán. The Mayas tried to vindicate their national personality in what was called 'La Guerra de las Castas', the War of the Castes. It began with a massacre of the mestizo and Spanish Creoles in the town of Bacalar in what is now the state of Quintana Roo. The Mayas were successful in driving out the non-Mayas from most of Yucatán, until the beleaguered city of Mérida was the only place inhabited. It is a sad tale of the efforts of a nation to preserve its self-determination. Mexico became stronger as the nineteenth century progressed, and so the Maya cause was lost. The survivors of the reprisals became politically listless corn farmers, theoretically free citizens of the Mexican republic.

They were able to maintain themselves for years by adopting guerrilla methods, obtaining supplies of guns and ammunition from the merchants of Belize City, to whom they sent mahogany which they floated down the Rio Hondo. The outside world has never heard of this episode in western history, and Mexico would like to forget it; but it had the effect of transferring from Yucatán to British Honduras a large number of mestizos, who fled from the Indians, and after them, a number of Indians, who fled from the Mexican authority. They first settled in the district of Corozal in the north of the Colony, where they built a little town of whitewashed adobe houses. In 1855 the population of the Colony was only 15,000; in 1861 it rose to 25,000 owing to the influx from the north.

The outbreak of hostilities had been caused by the Santa Cruz Indians who were favourably disposed to the Colony; but they were inveterate enemies of the Ycaiches, who were ready to attack both Mexicans and British impartially. After the massacre at Bacalar in 1848, things quietened down, until in the 1850s there was hope of peace and progress; but in 1857 the Chinchen-ha Indians, urged on by the Ycaiches, attacked the Colony, pillaging and demanding ransoms. A local leader arose, a national hero, not a bandit chief, whose name was Marcus Canul. In 1870 he and his men attacked the town of Corozal, but failed to hold the place, as the Santa Cruz Indians came to the rescue. Then from 18th to 30th August, 1872, Marcus Canul and about 150 Ycaiche Mayas crossed the Rio Hondo at Corozalito. They advanced deep into the territory of the Colony and attacked Orange Walk, 40 miles south of the Rio Hondo, near to which the new sugar refinery is now rising among the cane fields. The trouble had been anticipated; there was a small earth work called Fort Cairns Barracks, holding some 40 men of the West India Regiment, under the command of an English lieutenant, Smith, and a sergeant with the auspicious name of Belizario. This platoon held off the Indians for a whole day, with a loss of two men killed and 15 wounded, among whom was Lieutenant Smith. Sergeant Belizario then led a sortie against the attackers, and in the fight Marcus Canul was mortally wounded. His devoted men carried him from the field, and fought off the pursuit. He died that same night, and the Maya cause died with him. The survivors of the band, who had 15 killed and several wounded, did not return to Mexican territory, but settled in the Colony, where no one molested them, and where their descen-dants live peaceful and useful lives as Maya-Belizeans.

To these immigrations we owe the foundation of a group of villages in the extreme west of the Colony, Benque Viejo del Carmen, San Ignacio del Cayo and Succotz, inhabited by Mayas and mestizos, who have forgotten their ancestral discord. The Maya language survives, but is giving way before the Spanish of the mestizo; both tongues are fading before the English of primary education. There has been much admixture between the mestizos and the Indians, so it is now impossible to say whether a man is a real Indian, which he may claim to be and whose language he may speak, or a mestizo living in an Indian village. Some Creoles have reached this district; and the Lebanese have been there for three generations, and have bred with the original settlers, until now the threads are so interwoven that they are untraceable. All share equally their loyalty to the British Crown, and their enthusiasm for the new state of Belize, for they are keenly conscious of their common nationality.

Through the village of Succotz the Mopan runs to join the Belize River a few miles below. It is a stretch of deep green clear water between some very broken rapids. Maya boys fish there with spears, standing like statues on the brink with weapon poised. A Creole boy, who was sitting in his underpants at the ferry was asked how deep the stream might be. In reply he dived straight down, and came up saying that he could not reach bottom; so it must be 20 feet or more. Shoals of minnows swam all around the ferry, which was a flat-decked barge on a wire cable, capable of carrying a three-ton vehicle. This contraption is carried over by a winch and a gear wheel, and is free of charge until nine o'clock at night, when the ferryman can demand a fee, which is his, not the government's.

A mile past the ferry is Xunantunich, where the best-known Maya pyramids have been excavated and dressed up for tourism. The name is not the original, which has been totally forgotten for 800 years, but when the Mayas from Mexico settled here in the last century they called the place by that name. On a hilltop overlooking the valley of the Mopan River, the ancient Mayas levelled off the summit, and there erected a group of pyramids. There is a plaza of about an acre in extent, with four pyramids, oriented to each true cardinal point. Behind the southern pyramid there is another plaza of about the same size, with a pyramid on the eastern side, and the remains of public buildings along the others. When excavation was begun, these pyramids were covered with trees, some of which were a yard thick; but the vegetation has been cleared, and two of the pyramids reveal approximately their original features, which included steep stairways up the main faces. A band of frieze-work carving has been restored to its original condition. When the place was alive with people it must have been a most beautiful group of buildings, and the stone carvings of white rock in the strong sunlight must have been most conspicuously visible. The details of the carving are ugly, however artistic they may be, and exciting to archaeologists; they portray the most repugnant faces of demons that the frightened Mayas could imagine and still glare with hate and menace.

The late Mr. A. H. Anderson, the archaeologist of the Colony, who devoted 20 years of his life to discovering the secrets of Xunantunich, built stairways up the pyramid, and supplied stout ladders where stairs cannot be cut, so that one can reach the top with relative ease. From there one has a marvellous view across the valley, with the hills of Petén to the west, falling away to the east towards the flat of the coast. I remarked on the advantages of the site as a lookout station; and Mr. Anderson had the very reasonable theory that the pyramids, in addition to their religious function, served as 'telegraph' towers, with perhaps a system of smoke signals. The remains of the buildings around the plaza have so crumbled and decayed by erosion and the growth of tree roots that they cannot be restored. What remains is a very thick-walled, small-roomed place. I offer my own little contribution to Maya archaeology by saying that they were the cells of the town gaol. Certainly they would need only a minimum of reconstruction to be a good police-station basement.

Along the western highway from Belize City to Benque Viejo del Carmen there are many mounds, not as high as a two-storey house, which seem to be artificial, and must hide more Maya ruins. There is scope for archaeological excavation for scores of years to come, for all over the country, except on the barren sandy heath behind Belize City, there are ruins scattered in the bush. To realize what happened since the heyday of the Maya, we must imagine a country which, once as densely populated as modern agricultural areas of England and Scotland, reverted to forest by desertion of all the inhabitants, with the site of St. Paul's Cathedral a mound overgrown with brambles, and the Houses of Parliament a reef of rocks in the middle of a swamp. Some original Mayas still occupied the country when the Spaniards discovered the coast, as the Maya names of the rivers show. By the middle of the seventeenth century they had evacuated British Honduras, and did not return until the middle of the nineteenth, but the present Mayas of the Colony do not number one hundredth of their ancestors.

The Royal Ontario Museum of Toronto, Canada, is undertaking the excavation of another Maya site about 30 miles north of Belize City. It is an area of about seven or eight square miles thickly studded with mounds, which must have been more important as a centre than Xunantunich. All is forgotten, and the name has vanished with the people. It is known as Rockstone Pond, from a 'cenotl', or sink hole in the limestone rock, which measures perhaps two acres in extent. This was translated into modern Mopan Maya as Altun Ha, for tourism purposes. The usual group of pyramids has been identified around a square plaza and a score of lesser mounds await pickaxe and spade. Experienced Mayan workmen from Succotz, who have been trained by the late Mr. Anderson, are scraping the dirt off the principal pyramids under the supervision of Dr. David Prendergast, an American archaeologist from the University of Utah.

Altun Ha is not open to the public as the work is far from complete. In the first months of the excavation no approach road had been opened up. To get there one had to go along a mile of track that in the wet season only a four-wheel-drive vehicle could negotiate. At the main site there is a well-built cane and thatch house where the archaeologists live, with Mrs. Prendergast as head cook and bottle washer. The pyramid was a heap of loose boulders, whatever casing it might have had having long since disintegrated. The gentle sea breeze which tempered the heat on level ground was a raging gale at the peak. Dr. Prendergast was enthusiastic. He had opened a tomb with oyster shells inside, and has a theory that the Mayas were a sea-going people, and also deep sea divers, as the shells belong to a species of oyster that grows only in deep water.

Modern Maya workmen were scraping carefully through the platform to redeem bits of pottery bowls. To build the pyramid the planners first made a platform, and then packed earth on the top. Then they proceeded with another platform on that, and so on until the last step of the pyramid was too small to have more than a shrine or small temple with an altar – or a signal station for smoke signals. In the earth of the platforms they had trampled down were the broken bowls that once held their lunches. None of the pieces was larger than a half-crown, and none seemed to be other than kitchenware.

In the south of British Honduras near Punta Gorda there are other Maya sites, awaiting excavation under government supervision; their value as tourist attractions is well recognized. In this district also there live Mayas of the Kekchi tribe, who are far less assimilated than the Succotz Maya, and they preserve their peculiar characteristics. They had absorbed a certain tinge of

Spanish culture before emigrating from Guatemala in the last years of Queen Victoria's reign, and their villages usually have names of saints; but the Spanish language has been lost. They formerly spoke only their own tongue, but are learning English, which will no doubt replace their dialect in due course. Primary education is in English and is a very strong solvent.

We set out in a Land-Rover with Mr. Faustino Zúniga as our interpreter. Mr. Zúniga represented this district in the Legislative Assembly; but a long illness, from which he fortunately recovered, had prevented his re-election. He knew everyone and was welcomed by all. Our driver was a burly Carib, Mr. Stephen Moreira, who had a perpetual grin and found joviality even in the bumps we met.

Outside Punta Gorda the countryside is well settled and has fenced fields and orchards. It produces rice, vegetables, cattle and pigs for Belize City. How the legend arose that in the Colony one can only get tinned food to eat, is a mystery. Everywhere we ate locally produced food, except for condensed milk in tea, and canned peaches for dessert. Near Punta Gorda a planted stand of timber is a government experiment with pines; it has not prospered as was hoped, and the plantation is to be abandoned owing to indifferent growth.

The first Kekchi village, San Pedro Colombia, 19 miles west of Punta Gorda, can be reached by a decent road. It consists of a score of wooden houses with thatched roofs, straggling around a better built municipal office. A big Indian, very big for an Indian, as they are usually smallish folk, with a gold front tooth, presented himself and said in perfect English:

'The Chairman of the village, gentlemen. What can I do for you?' Mr. Zúniga spoke to him about official matters in Kekchi, and Mr. Moreira asked me if I wanted to meet an American couple, who were working in the place for the Peace Corps. We went to a house, indistinguishable from the rest of the cottages from whose doors bare breasted Indian housewives gazed at us; surrounded by a swarm of Indian children we shook hands with an elderly couple. The lady gave Mr. Moreira some packets of vegetable seeds that she had promised him on a previous visit.

'How do you get on with the Americans here?' I asked Mr. Zúniga.

'Why, with the very best of friendship,' he replied. 'They are some of the nicest people, and so ready to help. The lady has learnt embroidery from the Indian women, and the gentleman so likes life here that when his time is finished with the Peace Corps, he says he intends to arrange his affairs in the United States of America and come back here to live.'

One could well appreciate this. To retire to a place with a pleasant climate, with intelligent, friendly people around, with an absorbing intellectual hobby – studying the Kekchi language – and with living expenses at a minimum, what more could a sensible man want?

San Miguel is two miles deeper into the interior and is a village very like San Pedro Colombia. The school is a boarded shed with earth floor, but moderately sufficient in furniture. Two Carib teachers, a man and a schoolmistress, teach 73 Indian children. They write the lessons on the blackboard in English, and then expound it in Kekchi, and go back to English. This method is making all the younger generation bilingual, and will kill the Kekchi language in the end; but it is inevitable. All the children stood up and chorused in English, 'Good morning, Sir', and when we left they sang out, 'Goodbye, Sir'.

The countryside became less cultivated, and began to get hilly, broken up into steep valleys with streams at the bottom of each. The road started to develop patches of mud that tried the Land-Rover's qualities to the utmost. The next place, San Antonio, was until a few years ago quite unreachable except by paddling a canoe up a river, and then mounting on a mule; but that wonderful modern invention the bulldozer, has made it easily attainable by land.

San Antonio, a most interesting place, is a large village, almost a small town, of about 1,200 people, all Maya Indians except for the family of village schoolteachers, who are Caribs, and the parish priest, Fr. John Paul Cull, a Jesuit, whose father was American and mother Mexican. He tears over the roads in his jeep, without which he could scarcely manage to visit his cluster of villages, and has to be his own mechanic. He took us to see the church and schoolhouse.

It was unusual to find in a remote part of Central America a well-built church of limestone with a belfry tower, and at the side a stone schoolhouse for 240 pupils and eight teachers. These Indians lived in Petén in Guatemala, but emigrated to British

Honduras about three generations ago. They first settled about five miles from the frontier at Pueblo Viejo (Old Town, in Spanish), and then some of them moved on to found San Antonio. They built themselves a wooden church, and to equip it with images of saints and bells they removed these from San Luis in Petén. In due course the people of San Luis Petén came over to recover the bells and saints; but they were sent away empty handed, and the church property remained in San Antonio. Naturally, it was feared that such an episode would attract the vengeance of Heaven, and in due course the wooden church of San Antonio was hit by lightning and burnt to the ground, and the saints' images being wooden were burnt as well. The bells were saved.

The Bishop decided that the bells should stay in San Antonio, and the villagers asked him to help them to have a real church, proof against the vagaries of Providence.

'You build a school of stones,' instructed the Bishop, 'and I guarantee that you will have help to build a church afterwards.'

So the Indians set to and built a school of local limestone, well constructed and ample for the children they bring into the world so frequently. They quarried the stone with hand tools, made their own lime and mortar, and went to the Bishop and told him they had done it.

'Splendid,' said the Bishop. 'Now you can quarry the stone for a church, and I have donations to pay two masons on full-time salaries.' Up went the church in no time, which gives a better insight into how the ancient Mayas built their pyramids than all the speculations of the archaeologists.

The church is dedicated to San Luis Rey, and the raid on San Luis in Petén should be regarded as rather a transfer of that saint to San Antonio, not as a piratical foray. Probably the Mayas of San Antonio considered that they were the real owners of the saints' images and the bells. There are eight stained glass windows, and on examination showed a peculiarity. The saint, St. John, is identified in English, but along the bottom edge of the window is a line in German: 'Andenken an Heinrich Koop'. The next window is the same – a saint named in English with a line in German – 'Andenken an Heinrich Schuette'. Another is 'Andenken an Theodor Pietig', but the fourth is in English: 'Memorial to the Rev. Edward Wiggins 187–', but the last year

of the date is hidden under the edge of the framing. Five of the
eight windows are German memorials and three English.

No stained glass had been contemplated when the church
was planned; the openings in the walls were not quite the size
of the glass, and hence the incomplete date of the late Wiggins.

'A member of the Order was walking down a street in St.
Louis, Missouri,' related Fr. Cull, 'when he saw a church about
to be demolished with the headache ball on a crane arm. He
saw the windows in place, which nobody had wanted to buy
or even accept as a gift, and they were to go down with the rest.
So he begged them off the demolition company, and he got the
windows out unbroken. Someone donated the freight charges
to San Antonio, and here we installed them.'

Pueblo Viejo was the first settlement of the Kekchi and was
founded about 1866. It is a village of about 400 people. The
school has a roll call of 65, with one master, a Carib, who teaches
all forms. The scholars all stood up and chorused: 'Goodbye,

Swinging matchets – a traditional dance, Belize District.

Sir,' in English. They did not seem to be 65 in number, and the
master explained that influenza was keeping many away. It was
true. Half the people of the place were sneezing and coughing –
quite an epidemic.

We left Pueblo Viejo at midday and went to Santa Elena,
about four miles along the way back to San Antonio. I managed
to stay in a house long enough to examine the place in some
detail. It was a cottage, about five or six yards square, with a
good thatched roof of palm fronds, quite waterproof. The walls
were made of upright planks of mahogany, cut not with a saw
but by splitting the log with wedges. They were not trimmed,
and the chinks of light between the edges of the planks let in
fresh air. The furniture was simple and scanty. Beds were
made of low frames set in the earthern floor, over which was
spread a sheet of spongy bark from the 'moho' tree, thick and
soft like cork. These beds do service as tables, with small stools
to sit on. There were hammocks hanging all around, slung back
to the walls. The kitchen was an open fireplace in a corner, and
there was an ordinary kitchen table with a meat mincer used
for grinding maize for tortillas. Usually the Indians have a
saddle quern to grind the grain, but this is becoming obsolete.

There were bananas in bunches hanging from the beams.
Some sacks, labelled 'Coffee of Madagascar', proved to be full
of maize cobs, and others of beans. The place was full of food;
outside chickens and pigs were swarming. They were well
nourished and chubby people, and their children were innumerable.

The housewife was dressed in an embroidered blouse and a
blue skirt, rather longer than the present fashion would demand.
She was rather more dressed than most of the women who came
in to chat, clad in only their skirts. All of them wore bead neck-
laces and gold earrings, but no other ornaments, and no shoes.
Our hostess was 20 years of age and had four children. Another
woman present was 17 and had two children. These women
reach puberty at about the age of nine or 10, rarely as late as 11,
and they begin their procreative life at 12 or 13. When one
begins so early one must naturally end early as well. Eight or
10 children will be born to a woman before she is 30, and then
she is considered old. Of the family she may raise five, if she is
lucky and the children are robust. It may seem sad to us to burn

out so soon, but it is an accepted condition of life among the Kekchi Mayas, and they are not mournful.

The housewife had been sitting on a low stool before one of the beds, which was doing duty as a table, and on which she had placed her sewing machine, one of those hand-driven models, manufactured 60 years ago. She was making herself a new skirt. It was a good rayon cloth of light blue, which must have cost at least 10 shillings a yard, perhaps even more. The rest of her wardrobe was hanging over a hammock: 10 or 12 blouses and skirts, of good materials, nicely ironed; and her husband's shirts and trousers of cotton drill, well washed and ironed, were hanging there too.

The blouses were all hand-embroidered, which the women do themselves without tracing any design or pattern previously on the cloth. A blouse like this can be bought by arrangement; the average price will be 12 dollars or £3. The art is not commercialized yet, but the Tourist Section in Belize is contemplating selling these typical 'huipiles', as they are called in Maya, to the tourists from the north. Formerly all clothing was made of homespun cotton, and vegetable dyed thread was spun by hand for the embroidery, but now imported artificial silks have replaced the ancient crafts.

The influenza epidemic of Pueblo Viejo had arrived at Santa Elena, although infection was not so widespread. In one house both husband and wife were laid up in hammocks, both running high temperatures; and he, poor man, had an old sinus infection, which had asserted itself at the time. The Indians have their own herbal remedies which seem better than anything out of a chemist's shop for simple illnesses; they can find febrifuges among the common weeds of the hedgerow, but with a severe illness they have either to recover by themselves or die. Although there is a good hospital in Punta Gorda, the problem would be to get an injured or acutely sick person out over those appalling roads.

Financial conditions of the village are good. The Indians produce an agricultural surplus which they can now sell to dealers who deliver the produce to Belize City. As a result, many have a wad of banknotes hidden in the house. The local market is in San Antonio, where there is the shop from which the cloth for the dresses had come. It sells shotgun cartridges from

England, frying pans from Alabama, rayons from Japan and cottons from Hong Kong. The owner is a Maya. He has a small van to convey goods from Punta Gorda, buying from the wholesalers in Belize City for cash, and his inventory must be about $BH15,000 or nearly £4,000 sterling; with the premises and the van he must be worth £6,000 at least.

The Mayas of Punta Gorda district are by no means bedraggled ethnological curiosities, but comprise a vigorous and progressive group of Belizeans, quite aware of what is going on around them. Their chief contact with the outside world is through Caribs of Punta Gorda, who treat them with courtesy and kindness, and with whom they are on the best of terms.

8. MAHOGANY AND PINE

THE coat of arms of the Colony of British Honduras has the motto: 'Sub Umbra Floreo', with two woodcutters supporting the design. The concession from the Spanish Government to cut wood along the coast gave origin to the settlement of Belize and for 200 years timber remained its reason for existing. The first explorers found streams running through beautiful woods of huge trees, and most plentiful of all was mahogany.

These were not the original trees of tropical America. The abundance of mahogany dates from the clearing of the land by the Mayas. Those corn farmers stripped all forest cover off the clay where the primitive vegetation may have been quite different from that which the white men found. The Mayas needed breadnut for food, sapodilla for fruit and gum, cohune palm for oil and thatching, and mahogany for shade and timber. These species are found in greater proportion than the other trees in the reborn forests, and there are traces of Mayan agriculture in relation to this increase.

When overcrowding caused food shortages, the Mayas began to experiment with intensive as opposed to 'milpa' cultivation. They terraced the sides of the hills, and planted mahogany trees to keep the soil cool and shady, and on those terraces they tried out fertilizers. Remains of fish bones, spines of rays and other marine creatures have been found in the soil of the old terraces, and it has been surmised that seaweed carried up in baskets from the shore was used as manure. Tropical heat and rain will soon leach all the goodness out of an exposed soil. To be able to indulge in permanent agriculture, the soil must remain at a temperature of 77 degrees Fahrenheit or less, and to keep the temperature down, the Mayas thus planted belts of mahogany. After the fall of the civilization these terraces were neglected; and many were lost by erosion, together with the soil; but vestiges were preserved to distinguish the general plan.

Intensive agriculture was a new-fangled idea with the Mayas; they failed to appreciate its possibilities. When the authority of those who were experimenting came to an end, the art was forgotten. Mayas who remained reverted to their ancestral milpa, needing a large proportion of fallow to the area under productive cultivation. The forest cover did not replace itself as rapidly as was necessary to preserve the soil, and large parts of the country were so eroded that the topsoil was washed away, leaving bare limestone. The humus in the forest of today is still very thin – only six or nine inches, representing the formation of 1,000 years.

The first attempts at cutting were undertaken in the middle of the sixteenth century. But it was the valuable logwood for dyeing that attracted the Baymen at first. Mahogany was cut for ship repairing, and was soon recognized as fine timber because of the straightness and closeness of the grain. Trees grew all along the river banks; it was easy to fell them into the water, wait for the rainy season to swell the stream and then collect the logs at the sea shore. The supply of riverside timber was soon exhausted; but in the middle of the next century, by about 1670, slave labour had been introduced and made it feasible to cut farther back from the banks, using oxen to haul the logs to the stream. The penetration by the Scottish loggers with their crews of negroes into what was regarded by the Spaniards as their own private yard began the 200-year-long struggle for control of the territory.

As supplies were cropped the loggers had to go deeper into the hinterland to obtain the trees that were economically worth while. Only the larger trees, over a yard thick, could make it profitable, as the costs rose every year. At first mahogany was cut for shipbuilding only, but the loggers chopped down every logwood tree, size being of no importance as the logs were macerated to obtain the dye. The work became seasonal, the wet ground of the forest floor making it impossible to drag out the trunks during the rains; the loggers had to utilize the short dry season for that purpose. All depended on transport to the coast, and the only stands of any value were those that grew near enough to water.

On a likely place on the bank the operator would set up a temporary camp for himself and his crew. To reach the camp in those days there was only one route, by river; and so they would paddle their canoes up the Belize, or the New, or the Hondo.

During this voyage they would note the high water mark, shown by the line of stranded driftwood along the banks, and gauge the clearance of the rocks of the numerous rapids and shoals. On this calculation, which had to be done by expert, experienced men, depended the success of the 'drive' to the tidal water.

During the trip three or four 'hunters' would penetrate into the woods to see if the density of trees was sufficient to warrant cutting. Each tree counted would be blazed with a mark to identify it and avoid errors in counting. When the approximate number of trees available had thus been verified, the hunters would cut a base trail through the area, and from this line they would cut at right angles other trails, and subsequently auxiliary trails through the blocks of forest to the individual trees. Notched sticks were planted at the junctions of the trails to indicate the number of trees in each direction.

After this the semi-permanent camp of the cutters would be built. All the camp materials had to be cut during the week after a full moon, or else, it was said, the termites would eat up the houses; the superstition is still alive to this day. Frames were of timber, walls of bamboo and roofs of palm leaf thatch; they must have looked very like the Kekchi Maya houses of our time. The only method of securing the beams and walls and roofs was by tying them with wild vines, which abound in the bush. Then a place had to be made for the fodder for the oxen – essential for hauling logs to the waterside. The operator would then return to the coast to obtain supplies, such as salt pork and flour, and to recruit labour. Men were indentured for six months of the season, paid partly in advance, which enabled them to have a good orgy in Belize before leaving for the interior. Cutting would begin in December.

The chief problem of the loggers was to get the lumber to the waterside as cheaply as possible. If the trees grew near the river they could be rolled down the bank by leverage; but if they were farther away from the stream the costs rose, until they made operations uneconomical. A five-mile haulage by the ox-drawn sled or low truck, known by the Spanish word 'camión', was the limit of feasibility. A greater distance was too expensive. The mahogany tree develops in its maturity great buttresses at the roots, and to avoid these the fellers would have to erect a scaffolding about ten feet high round the trunk. Once the tree was down, the trunk would be cut through with cross-cut saws, until it was reduced to logs about 20 feet long, and perhaps two yards thick at the butt end. To get these enormous pieces out of a boggy forest required the efforts of four, eight or more yoke of oxen. The trucks had two, four, six or eight wheels, according to the size of the tree to be moved.

When the rains came it was necessary to make use of every storm, so that the rise in the level of the river could take the trunks over the rapids. If the swollen currents were not used, the opportunity was lost, and the logs would lie stranded until the next freshet. The loggers made deliveries at the 'boom', an artificial barrier at the mouth of the river, where the shippers picked up the wood for storage on board the ships. No sawing into boards and pieces was attempted until quite modern times. In 1933 the first sawmill was established in Belize City.

Today methods of handling have completely changed. No oxen haul logs and no axes chop down trees. Only one company of the Baymen survives. It cuts lumber by mechanical means. Bulldozers with the strength of 600 horses cut the trails through the bush, throwing two-foot-thick trees aside like matchsticks. Graders build up roads, and Land-Rovers skip with ease over these highways. The trees are felled by portable saws in a matter of minutes, and the tractors drag out three trees at a time. Very little of the lumber is exported as logs or rough hewn baulks, as it saves freight to saw on the spot. All this, however, means a very high investment in equipment that wears out quickly. When West African mahogany entered the market, the competition so lowered the price that three of the principal companies operating in British Honduras went out of business, but several smaller companies are now operating successfully. Today the dealers complain that the profits on lumber are too low to be worth while, despite which their handling of the commodity averaged nearly £600,000 a year between 1961 and 1965.

The earliest known figures for mahogany exports show that in 1802 2,280,000 board feet were shipped. (A board foot equals one-twelfth of a cubic foot.) Production wavered between two and six million board feet yearly during most of the nineteenth century, representing the maximum amounts that could be cut in the circumstances. In the 1840s the figure rose to over 10,000,000 board feet a year, as the railway industry called for much of this wood for building carriages, and the price rose with the demand. At the beginning of the present century there arose a demand for mahogany in the United States, causing a small boom, and the amount increased yearly to 16,000,000 board feet (1.3 million cubic feet) in 1914.

The chief difficulty in the trade was to get the wood out. The obstruction of granite outcrop at Little Falls on the Belize River was dynamited in 1905 and the branch of the Haulover Creek was widened and deepened so that in 1906 a launch could sail from El Cayo to the sea. The trip, which formerly took from 10 to 30 days, could now be made in 30 hours.

Meanwhile, the extraction of greater quantities of lumber by modern methods, and the reckless cutting without replanting, had so lowered stocks that the industry was almost extinct by 1922. The last stand of natural mahogany forest was at the frontier with Petén, 90 miles west of Belize City, where a lumber camp, Gallon Jug, was established at the terminus of a light railway running down to the New River at a point where a lake fills a natural depression, called Hill Bank. The wood was carried by the railway to this lagoon, and carried 180 miles by lake, river, and estuary to the saw mill on Haulover Creek in Belize City. In a straight line Hill Bank is 50 miles from the port, but roadless swamps intervene.

In 1965 Gallon Jug was abandoned; only two caretakers live there today. All the equipment was removed to Hill Bank Lagoon and set up afresh to cut over the stand of second growth at that place. Cutting takes place every 30 years. Hill Bank was cut over in the 1930s and the cement foundations of the manager's house can still be seen among the weeds, as obsolete a relic as a Maya pyramid. The new quarters of the administrative staff are going up some distance away. A road has been cut through the low bush, and as soon as the forest floor is dry enough to bear the loaded trucks, the lumber will flow out under strict government supervision.

The law does not normally allow a mahogany tree to be cut unless it is seven feet six inches thick at the base. But since many trees reach maturity before arriving at that size, and others develop defects, such as crookedness, not all the trees felled are so big. No trees other than mahogany are cut, except for some

'Spanish cedar', a lighter wood; the tree is a relative of mahogany the leaves being very similar in shape, and larger. When freshly cut the wood has a faint smell reminiscent of true cedar. This is due to a pungent oil in the cells of the wood, which is not to the taste of termites. That is why cedar is good for building and for furniture in the tropics. If the trees are large enough they are exported, but the lesser logs are sawn for local consumption.

To go along the rough logging road, which runs five miles northwards from the railhead at Hill Bank, is a revealing experience. One speaks of not seeing the wood for the trees. Here it is a question of not seeing the trees for the wood. The forest is a mass of creepers and bushes with worthless lesser growth screening everything. Only an expert forester or lumber-man could move 20 yards without being lost in this thicket. The soil, a mass of soggy decayed vegetable matter, is alive with leeches. It is neither romantic nor beautiful – only unpleasant. Very few birds live in the shade, and the animals come out only at night-time. It provides very little wild fruit or other food for a human being, and depresses the spirits. It is with a sense of relief that one returns to the group of sheds that form the settle-ment at the temporary sawmill by the lagoon.

The mahogany of British Honduras is almost exhausted. The original concession made to the Baymen by the Spanish Crown was to cut trees along the banks of the rivers between the Belize and the Hondo rivers, that is to say, in the northern half of the present Colony. Not a tree is to be found there now. Mahogany cannot grow on the limestone and sandy flats, where only pines will sprout. Some stands still exist in the centre of the country, such as Hill Bank, but the last sanctuary is the Chiquibul Forest Reserve on the Maya Mountains in the south-central districts.

This is an area of 720 square miles of government-owned land, in which private cutting is licensed. To get there one leaves the Western Highway, before arriving at the experimental station for agriculture at Central Farm, 60 miles west of Belize City, and takes a road to the left. The rolling countryside of farm and cattle ranch soon gives way to land broken by the deep gullies of small streams; then one enters the Mountain Pine Ridge Forest Reserve. This is a tract of 282 square miles of pine woods. The land is a sandy heath, with at most a few inches of gravel over the limestone. The granite bones beneath this lean flesh protrude as vast boulders and outcrops. Erosion has carried off the soil after many forest fires, and the limestone will disappear in time. Chemical action of the air has rounded the granite blocks. The only trees are pines, and the only undergrowth is grass. Grazing is rented out and 3,000 head of cattle are doing reasonably well.

From the road one cannot see any trees of large size, although there are some of cuttable size in the interior. Those near the road range in size from an ordinary Christmas tree to about 12 feet in height and cannot be more than a few years old.

About 15 miles inside the forest is the Forestry Department Station. Their chief activity is fire-fighting, at which they have become expert. The settlement was named after Augustine, a mestizo from El Cayo, who used to live there all alone. What happened to the original 'Augustin' has never been discovered. He disappeared, and probably died in the forest, and his bones must moulder in some cranny. His ghost is said to haunt the place, and his howls at night are indistinguishable from the soughing of the wind in the pines.

No replanting is being attempted in the Mountain Pine Ridge Reserve. The propagation of the trees is left to natural regeneration.

From the Station, which consists of about 20 board houses with a school and a community recreational centre, the road runs down to the bed of the Chiquibul River. On the way is the village of San Luis, where the concessionaire has established a sawmill. The licence to cut in the Chiquibul Forest is in the hands of Wahib Habet and his family, Lebanese citizens of Belize; and at the mill was Mr. Salvador Habet, a burly man with a black beard. Careful tally is taken of the trees marked by the forestry experts before felling; the amounts of lumber obtained are noted so that statistics of the productivity of the various soils can be recorded. No mahogany was being cut at the time; the only lumber drying out in the yards was cedar.

Beyond the camp the road becomes miry and foul in the extreme as it is cut up by the 15-ton trailers which haul the trunks out of the forest. The monsters hurry past leaving ruts a yard deep in the clay. Five miles farther on one reaches the Chiquibul River, running between deeply cut banks and bluffs, over a bed of boulders that divide the body of the stream into a hundred courses. A low concrete bridge has been built, strong enough to take the weight of a truck with three logs, but in the rainy season it must surely disappear under the flood. Past the river the scenery changes completely with a suddenness that is almost disconcerting. The pines cease as if by magic and the soil is now a deep clay. The vegetation is a mass of trees and creepers, and tall trees can be seen over the heads of the lesser growth. This is not high bush, which is found 10 miles deeper in the reserve; but it is true tropical forest, with tapirs and deer, and jaguars and pumas. The only visible animals were three mules, which must have strayed from the grazing grounds of the more open Mountain Pine Ridge.

An occasional stump of a cedar or mahogany tree can be seen from the road, if road it can be called, for it is a most frightful ditch of mud, along which even a Land-Rover with its four-wheel drive can scarcely travel. In this forest the 'chicleros' wander, gathering chicle, the gum of the sapodilla tree, which they boil at camping places, like gypsies at the side of the trail. They look very rough types, although, bathed and combed, they might be less frightening. Every man carries his shotgun on his shoulder as he wanders through the tangled woods, and a large part of his diet is wild meat obtained as he works. Most chicleros are Indians or mestizos, although an occasional Creole gets into the trade. They bring the semi-prepared gum to Messrs. Habet, who act as middlemen, selling the product to importers in England and the United States. If anyone could see a chicle encampment he would forswear chewing gum for the rest of his days.

No large trees are left near the trail. After penetrating into the Chiquibul Forest for several miles, we turned back, defeated by the mire, and retraced our tracks, looking for a place to park and eat our lunch. We searched in vain for suitable shade until we had recrossed the river by the bridge, and arrived again at Augustine. In 10 miles of road there was not a tree sufficiently tall to shade the Land-Rover.

The exhaustion of the mahogany has been a problem for the last century in British Honduras, but no real effort has been made to solve it. At one time the Assembly legislated that every time a tree was felled, the loggers must plant mahogany at the site; but the law could never be enforced, as it necessitated inspection and constant supervision of every felling site – a practical impossibility. The nature of the market had ensured that only large logs were extracted, and this made the 'creaming' operations highly selective.

When the trees had been felled the space left was not immediately replanted by mahogany saplings. The seeds found difficulty in rooting on the unprepared soil and regeneration was easier where the soil had been turned over by the wheels in the trails or the trampled logbeddings at the waterside or the abandoned temporary corn patches of the foresters.

When a large tree is chopped down the area formerly covered by its shade does not immediately sprout new trees. The first growth is of rank weeds, many poisonous and all useless. After the first year, bushes begin to crowd out the weeds; the new trees are not strong enough to suppress the bushes until the fifth year. Of the seeds that fall from a tree in season not one in 1,000 manages to sprout. Of the seedlings that do appear, not one in 10 survives the first year, and not one in 100 will finally become a monarch of the forest. It is a most wasteful and merciless process, meaning frustration and death to all but one reproductive effort in 100,000. When people say that they are relying on 'natural regeneration' to replenish the forests, they really are doing nothing whatsoever to replace what has been destroyed.

The result has been a gradual reduction in the growth of mahogany. To reverse this trend, the Forest Trust was created in 1923; this body carried out experiments between 1923 and 1925 in order to encourage the survival and growth of natural seedlings in selected areas. Most of these operations ceased by the early 1930s; but records showed that stocking of the forests was certainly increased. In the Silkgrass area mahogany saplings increased from 1.4 per acre in 1928 to 14.8 an acre in 1929. If this rate of increase had been maintained, the area today would be a rich mahogany forest, which it is not. Constant care and maintenance are necessary to bring a crop of mahogany to maturity; and therefore it is obvious that intensive plantation must take place and the costs concentrated. This policy was adopted for some years. In 1955 it was observed in the Chiquibul Forest that several thousand acres of good natural regeneration had occurred in areas burned over by an exceptionally large fire in 1945.

Then in the 1950s a new method was adopted in the Kekchi country. The Indians shift their 'milpas' every three or four years, leaving the fallow to go back to bush. They are allowed to farm in the Reserve by the Columbia River and, in return, plant mahogany seeds with their corn. By the third year there has been sufficient time for the mahogany to get a hold, as by then the trees are a yard tall. After the Indians have abandoned the sites, it is sufficient to clear the jungle growth around the saplings for two or three years, by which time they have enough strength of their own to push upwards. By the year 2035 there will be a magnificent mahogany forest there again, ready for scientific cutting. Thus does the wheel turn full circle. The mahogany forests brought into being by the frustrated intensive agriculture of the ancient Mayas are being re-created in the milpas of their descendants.

Good wood can only be produced by hereditary aristocrats who can afford to disdain the passage of time, or by a government which is not obsessed by the profit motive. Private operators in timber will not wait 80 years for the plantings to ripen, except in rare cases when a man will think of his grandchildren's welfare. When dividends for shareholders loom large in a manager's mind forestry suffers. There is a large stand of pine in British Honduras near Mango Creek, where the ill-fated factory for resin was erected by Hercules Powder Company. The private company that owns the land does not take the risk of cutting the trees on its own account, as fluctuations in the price of lumber overseas might make that profitless. Rather it prefers to offer the trees standing in the forest to private cutters at $BH3.50 each and purchase the lumber, which it saws in its own mill at Mango Creek at $BH70 1,000 board feet. The private operators say that they cannot make any profit at these prices, as the margin is too small to cover their costs. The result is that the stands of timber languish until the next forest fire sweeps them away. It is probable that in the not too distant past the Mountain Pine Ridge Reserve, which today is a waste of sand and rock, sparsely covered with pine and grass, was a mixed forest like the Chiquibul on the other side of the river. Fires denuded the land, and a very fierce fire can bake out of the land the bacteria essential even for the growth of weeds. The eroded soil was washed off by the rains and deposited in the wide bay that formerly occupied the sandy heath behind Belize City. On the rocks left uncovered, only the pines and the grass could re-establish themselves.

In 1965 total production of lumber amounted to 2.2 million cubic feet, though this was admittedly an exceptional year. It is probable that exports will level off in the next 10 years or so at about seven to 10 million board feet. There is no doubt that the timber industry is in decline, but the position need not be considered gloomy. Nowadays all timber is exported as lumber (sawn logs), whereas in the earlier days it was exported as logs. The establishment of sawmills has assisted the economy considerably.

9. SUGAR AND CITRUS

VERY early in the history of the territory sugar canes were introduced, probably from Jamaica. The demand was not for sugar, but for molasses to make rum. No refining was attempted, nor was it possible with the primitive methods then in use. The mills, called 'trapiches', consisted of three upright rollers of hard wood, moved by oxen, walking round and round in a circle, yoked to a long overhead beam. The operator had to pass the stalks two or three at a time between the rollers, and on the other side they were received by a second worker, who doubled the crushed stems over and repassed them through the mill. Many a man lost his fingers from carelessness in handling the cane. Small roller mills of this type, but of cast iron, can still be seen in many parts of Latin America.

Refugees from Yucatán, fleeing the Indian risings of 1848, came to Corozal in the north of British Honduras, and were invited by a Mr. James Blake to bring sugar cane with them and to settle on his land in that district. The cane was the Bourbon variety which, a century later, still grows in the Toledo District of British Honduras. Mr. Blake provided land and assistance to the settlers from Yucatán, and established a new crop. Cane planting spread south from Corozal in 1869, when American refugees from the southern states came to Toledo as a result of the American Civil War. Plantations were established at Regalia and Serpon in the Stann Creek District and at Seven Hills in the south. The plantations were about 400 acres each, and the yield is said to have been one and a half to two tons of sugar an acre.

All through the nineteenth century sugar and rum were exported from Belize to Central America, and in 1879, when statistics were first available, the annual export was worth $82,000. This was a very low figure, for in 1880 it rose to $234,000 and in 1881 it was $212,000. In that year the export weight of sugar was given as 1,902 tons.

In the last years of the nineteenth century prices began to fall, and the first quarter of the twentieth century saw an almost complete eclipse of production in British Honduras. Exports to Central America of sugar and rum fell to $40,000 in 1919, and almost disappeared at $12,000 in 1921. In 1933 only 500 tons were exported. The heavy rainfall in the Toledo district, over 100 inches a year on an average, caused very low returns of sugar from the cane. The last southern plantations were abandoned by 1935.

In 1937 a local company was formed and a mill was installed at Pembroke Hall, eight miles south of Corozal Town, and 87 miles north of Belize City. It was recently renamed Libertad. This was a modest installation of eleven 18 in. by 32 in. rollers, which could produce 3,000 tons of sugar a year, but it actually produced only about 1,200 tons a year for local consumption. The Colony had an export quota of 1,000 tons a year under the International Sugar Agreement of 1937, but this became inoperative on the outbreak of war in 1939.

The cane was provided by small growers, as the company did not at that time till its own fields. The yield was understandably low, as the planters were not accomplished agriculturists; they produced only 12 tons of cane per acre, compared with 40 tons per acre from scientific planting. However, the sugar content of the cane was high – one ton of sugar being extracted from between eight to eleven tons of cane. This showed that the land was fertile, and promised well for the future.

After the war the industry began to grow. More and more acres of cane were planted, incidentally causing an influx of Mexicans into Corozal District. The mill was enlarged, and in 1960 over 12,000 tons of sugar were exported to Britain under the Commonwealth Sugar Agreement. In 1961 this was more than doubled, no less than 27,577 tons being sent over. The average yield of sugar was one ton for every 8.83 tons of cane, which was very satisfactory. Production continued to rise. In 1963 over 30,000 tons were exported. In 1964 the factory was taken over by Messrs. Tate & Lyle Ltd.; they bought the shares of the company from the local and Jamaican shareholders, and then began a complete overhaul and modernization of plant and methods. In 1967 59,000 tons of sugar were produced, the goal being 75,000 tons for 1968 and 100,000 tons in 1970, if markets can be found for that quantity. The company is now known as Belize Sugar Industries Ltd.

To maintain these high production figures it had been necessary to place the business in the hands of new owners, who had the capital necessary for the increased investment, and to obtain the ammonium sulphate fertilizer from Trinidad, without which the larger yields would have been impossible. The mill was refurbished and much enlarged, and new warehouses were built in Belize City for the sugar pending export.

For miles around the mill, cane fields extend in unfenced 10-acre blocks. The company plants half the cane it needs on its own land, leases land for planting and buys cane from smaller growers.

Formerly cane was planted and cut by hand. The conventional picture of a sugar field always includes a line of men in broad brimmed straw hats, swinging machetes against the cane. One can still see this in some parts of the Libertad fields; but it will not be long before the humble 'Cañero' will disappear with the oxcart and the machete, as things of a laborious and underpaid past. There is no surplus labour in British Honduras; indeed, a satisfactory rate of development would not be possible unless maximum use was made of labour-saving techniques. Such techniques are becoming necessary to meet the increasingly competitive conditions in world sugar markets.

About a mile from the Belize Sugar Industries plant a huge machine was harvesting the cane. Near by, a gang of machetemen advanced slowly against a wall of green. Thus the relative merits

Boats in one of the typical creeks that feed the rivers.

and demerits of both systems were comparable. The machine was developed in Australia, where there are similar large fields and a lack of labour. It cost £12,000 and requires a crew of three men – the driver and two assistants. Whereas a good workman in the field can cut with his machete some four tons of cane a day, this machine will cut 250 tons, with the added advantage that the cane is delivered by the monster into a train of trailer trucks, reaching the mill half an hour after being cut. When cane is cut by hand, it stays on the ground waiting to be gathered. It may suffer some drying out, for it will probably not reach the mill until 24 hours later. The trailers will hold four tons of cane apiece; an oxcart will take perhaps half a ton at the most, and wear out the poor beasts that have to haul it.

The machine crept forward at less than walking pace. It gathered stalks of cane with a kind of fiendish energy into a cage in front, and then things like Archimedes screws cut the stalks at the root, and topped the trash of green leaves. Inside the machine the canes were sliced into three-foot lengths and spewed forth up a conveyor into the lorry alongside.

Sugar cane comes in many varieties. For this labour-saving machine, doing the work of 60 men under the supervision of only three, a special kind of cane has to be planted with special intervals between the rows. Sugar canes tend to grow crooked, leaning over almost horizontally, and then reaching upwards when they are somewhat thicker, seeking light and air in competition with their fellows. The result is often a semicircular stalk, which is not convenient for the machine; it would leave a lot of cane left on the field to be gleaned by hand, and the cost of gleaning would be so high that the cane were best left abandoned on the ground. So new canes have been bred, growing as straight as bamboo. This means replanting many thousands of acres of cane, which cannot be done in a short time. The cane is replanted every four years in British Honduras, undergoing three cuttings in the period, and until the time comes round for replanting, the old cane has to be left in the field.

The company has three of these machines and will import more of them in the future. It is not incorrect to say that without them the national income of the new nation of Belize would be considerably lower, as sugar is now the territory's principal export.

Once the cane is cut and carried to the mill it is dumped into a huge trench, the flooring of which is a moving band of wooden slats, 10 yards wide and 40 yards long, 10 feet deep at the end farthest from the plant itself. The cane arrives in bundles of about a ton a piece, bound with chains which have a shackle with a trigger attachment. Two men armed with iron-tipped poles poke the trigger as the bundles swing in the air, and the cane tumbles into the trench. There it moves very slowly forward to another conveyor belt set at right angles, much narrower, but running at a much higher speed. A revolving rake scrapes the heaps of cane into this and it disappears into the roller crushers.

The crushed cane passes through several sets of rollers until it is entirely deprived of any trace of juice, and is a fluffy whitish powder, called bagasse. This is not wasted, but is fed directly into the hoppers of the boilers to provide steam power. The juice runs into mysterious vats, disappearing completely from sight; but sundry knowing fellows keep track of it, peering through little glass peepholes in pipes and evaporating pans, which are not pans at all, but huge receptacles with thousands of gallons of juice in each.

The juice is then converted into a black thick substance, like tar; anything less apt for human consumption would be hard to imagine. Some of this gritty stuff slides reluctantly down into a big cup, about a yard high and a yard wide, and there it is whirled around at a tremendous speed and gradually becomes, by a kind of perpetual miracle, nice brown sugar. It is entrancing to watch the sticky mess turn lighter and lighter in colour. What happens is that the molasses is driven out by centrifugal force through screens of fine wire mesh, leaving the sugar dry and clean.

The brown sugar is not further refined in British Honduras, but is gathered into barges specially built for sugar transit; they lie in the New River alongside the mill. Everything is done by machinery. The only occasion when a hand touches the sugar in the whole process is when the operator of the centrifuge introduces a new batch of treacle into his machine. It slides down a wooden chute, and after he cuts off the supply he scrapes the end of the chute with a wooden paddle, so that no late gobs fall into the brown sugar below.

The rest of the story is in Liverpool, where the complete

refining of the sugar into white crystals and lumps is completed. The Colony produces only brown sugar for export.

In accordance with the long-range plan to increase sugar production in British Honduras, a new mill was constructed in 1965 and 1966 at Tower Hill, not far from the town of Orange Walk on the New River. This is 62 miles north of Belize City on the highway to Corozal. A mile before the plant site is reached one formerly had to cross the river by a cable-driven barge-ferry, but now a new bridge has been built to carry the road over the stream. Three hundred men were employed in the construction job, and 200 remain as permanent employees of the company. This is a very large establishment, with 9,000 acres of its own plantations and as it will purchase a similar amount from local growers, it is hoped that the newly created industry in the neighbourhood will be able without difficulty to absorb the men left over from the construction job.

About $BH24,000,000, equal to £6,000,000, has been invested in this enlargement of the sugar industry in British Honduras, and the result is very impressive. The repair workshop alone is an enormous building and looks as if it were capable of servicing a battleship.

The supply of cane is one of the first cares of the company. It is useless to spend several million pounds on a new sugar mill and then find that it cannot work at capacity for lack of material, like the unfortunate Hercules resin plant at Mango Creek. To avoid such a calamity, careful arrangements have been made under government supervision for the company to receive its full quota of cane, and the small growers in the district can also be assured of just treatment. The plan seems honest and fair. The company by law has to purchase half the cane it needs from smaller growers who deliver cane at the mill for a previously negotiated price, based on the price of sugar on the world market. Then after the production has been sold, the company will share 65 per cent of its profits on the deal with the growers.

No account of sugar cane planting in the Colony would be complete without just recognition of the improvements brought about by Government action in aiding the farmers. Sir Colin Thornley, Governor at the time of the hurricane of 1955, addressed cane planters at a meeting at Louisville on 10th October, 1955, and promised to assist them to organize an effective co-operative unit. The Cane Planters' Co-operative was formed in 1956 as a direct result of this action. However, the management of this co-operative left much to be desired, and so in 1959, after consultation with all sides concerned, the Government passed two important Ordinances (Nos. 12 and 13 of that year) to regulate the whole cane industry in the territory. In 1960 the first full-time Cane Farming Officer was employed, and seconded as an employee; he functioned as secretary of the newly formed Sugar Board created by the Sugar Industry (Control) Ordinance No. 12 of 1959.

Before 1960 there had been only a few simple fertilizer and variety trials carried out on sugar cane by the Government Agricultural Department. The Department had been under-staffed and a difficulty was the fact that the sugar cane area was some 150 miles from the Research Station. A well planned scheme of soil analysis, compilation of rainfall statistics, fertilizer needs, and the like, was got under way and the results were spectacular.

In 1954 British Honduras planted 3,416 acres of sugar cane which produced a crop of 21,318 tons reaped. This yielded 2,413 tons of sugar, or only seven-tenths of a ton an acre.

In 1964 the planting was over 14,000 acres, and the crop weighed 272,319 tons of cane, producing 33,591 tons of sugar. This is an average of 2.4 tons an acre, or more than three times the yield of 10 years previously. The Agricultural Department's efforts to improve the methods of planting and to introduce better varieties of cane had had notable success.

The citrus industry has many points in common with sugar in British Honduras, but also many essential differences. Both depend on overseas markets for the disposal of their products, and both are affected by world prices. In both cases there are large processers who have their own raw materials and are also the purchasers of the output of the small growers. But there the resemblance ends. A good part of the sugar is sold under a negotiated price (over twice the present world price) while citrus has to face cut-throat world competition.

As with coffee planting and other tropical cash-crops for export, citrus suffers from the fluctuations of prices over a cycle of years. When prices are high and growers are making handsome profits, there is a rush to plant new trees. These need some five years at least to enter into commercial production, by which time the glut on the market has caused prices to fall; an excess of supply over demand. The new plantations cannot then sell their crops at a price that will produce a yield high enough to satisfy the needs, and far less the hopes, of the enthusiastic growers. They are then inclined to blame the low prices, not on the world situation and surpluses, but on the sinister machinations of marketeers and processers.

Thus in British Honduras the tale was no different in essence from that of the coffee growers' plight in the rest of Central America. When oranges fetched $2.30 a box of 90 lb., which is the standard unit in the industry (grapefruit running at 80 lb. to the box), there was a great increase of citrus plantations in the Stann Creek District of British Honduras, and plantations began to be started in other parts, such as El Cayo District. Then world prices started to fall and reached $0.81 a box. The news of a cold wave in Florida, with the prospect of ruin for millions of boxes of fruit in that part of the United States of America, sent up hopes, which were dashed when Providence relented and sent the cold snap way back up north. The price was said to have recovered to $0.90 a box, and the prices locally in British Honduras did not react as the small growers would have liked. The processers were offering $0.83 or even $0.85, but the small growers did not believe this was a just price for their fruit.

The matter being of vital economic importance to about 200 small growers, who were utterly dependent on the processers and exporters for the sale of their crops, tempers became inflamed and a serious situation could have developed. The Government took steps to deal with the critical situation. Consultations were held with everyone concerned. The result was the presentation of a Bill for an Ordinance to regulate and control the citrus industry, not to dictate but to provide both small and large growers and processers and exporters with a reasonable basis for the adjustment of any disputes. This became law in March 1967 as Ordinance No. 2 of 1967.

The Ordinance provides for a Citrus Control Board, composed of the Permanent Secretary to the Ministry of Natural Resources and the Chief Agricultural Officer, who are *ex officio* members; then there are two representatives of the processers, who shall be elected by the processers themselves, and two representatives of the Citrus Growers' Association, with three more members, who shall be persons having no connection with the citrus industry. The Secretary of the Ministry of Natural Resources is the Chairman of the Board.

The Board will issue licences to producers, who will be awarded basic quotas for deliveries to the processers, and of course keep records of the returns made by the producers. It will hear and determine appeals by any person who considers that he has a grievance to ventilate. The Board will determine every year the price per box of citrus to be paid by the processers to the producers and determine the payment to be made on delivery of the fruit to the processers, and the amount to be paid to complete the price after the fruit has been exported. The amounts will be calculated by taking into account the sale price of citrus, the quantities available and the value of by-products, such as orange oil.

The Ordinance provides for the liquidation of the former British Honduras Citrus Growers' Association, and its replacement by a Citrus Growers' Association, which will be the instrument to take care of the growers' interests. The difference between the two associations is that the new one will be under the control of the Chairman of the Board, in whose presence documents of the Association will be sealed. The Association has a wide scope and can import fertilizers and tools for the members, advance them money and generally act on their behalf without official interference. But the essential licensing does away with the danger of uncontrolled planting. The fixing of prices before the delivery season by common consent of processers and producers deals with some of the friction concerning the price to be paid.

This legislation can remove internal friction, but it cannot remedy low world prices for citrus products. However, it does reduce some of the disharmony between those who grow and those who buy the crops.

The history of citrus in the territory is not clearly defined, as no records are available. Citrus fruits are not native to America and were unknown to the Indians before the Spanish conquest. The first mention seems to be that of the planting of oranges near Campeche in what is now Mexico by the Conquistador Bernal Diaz del Castillo, about the year 1540. Logwood cutters operated in the Campeche district for a very long period, and some of them may have brought back orange seeds to what is now British Honduras. Limes were extensively grown in Central America by the Spaniards in the colonial period; this variety of citrus was more popular than oranges and lemons since the juice was used to make lemonade as a refreshment and as a preventive against scurvy in the ships' crews. When the habit of drinking orange juice for breakfast began in the United States of America early in the present century, orange cultivation received a tremendous impulse and became big business. According to the 'Archives' of Governor Burdon of British Honduras, the industry was really established on a commercial footing in 1912 or 1913 by 'two far-sighted gentlemen', one of them being related to one of the largest growers of today. The Jamaican firm of Sharpe Brothers Limited entered the industry in 1928, and the growth of the orange juice industry dates from the award of a 10-year contract by the British Ministry of Food in 1949–50.

Two firms control the industry. Both grow fruit on their own account, and both also purchase the crops of smaller plantations. The original Jamaican firm of Sharpe Brothers is now incorporated in the Citrus Company of British Honduras Limited, and a few years ago the Canadian firm, Salada Foods Inc. of Toronto, Ontario, purchased from the British Commonwealth Development Corporation 3,000 acres of citrus plantations in the Stann Creek District, and formed the British Honduras Fruit Company Limited.

The Salada Foods Company's plant is not a very large installation; it was erected and functioning in the record time of six weeks. It selects, washes, and squeezes oranges, and boils, concentrates, packs and freezes the juice. The plant can handle half a million boxes of 90 lb. each every season. The boxes are open crates piled full of fruit, and they wait at the side of the road until the lorry comes to carry them to the plant. There they are delivered by pouring the fruit on to a conveyor belt, consisting of a series of metal rollers separated by about half an inch of space, through which chinks the leaves, stalks and other waste fall to the ground. As the fruit is discharged checkers vigilantly spy out any bruised, damaged or unhealthy oranges, which are dropped into boxes alongside and go back to where they came from. It is a frequent complaint of the buyers that the smaller farms deliver fruit of inferior quality; this method makes it certain that the quality of the rejects can be noted afterwards.

The conveyor ends at a vertical band of buckets which scoop

the oranges upwards, and then dump them on to another horizontal band – a rubber belt, about a yard wide, which carries the fruit to the washer. While the oranges parade along this they are scrutinized again, and rejects are tossed into chutes that return them to the waiting lorry below. The washing machine drips soapsuds on to the oranges which are carried along slowly and deposit themselves on to a series of rollers that are really brushes. These scrub the soapy oranges while sprays of water rinse off the soap; and, as clean as children going to Sunday School, the fruit goes on to the presses.

There is a final scrutiny to eliminate any sinner that may have escaped the watchers along the line; the fruit is moved neatly into little passages along which only one orange can go at a time. Then up comes a cup, into which the orange falls and is carried over a quarter of a circle, until, with the swiftness of a leaping jaguar, another cup comes down, over the cup holding the orange, which then ceases to be an orange, as pressure forces the juice out. It is a mechanism rotating on an axle, and after the squeezing has been accomplished, the lower cup continues round the circle; gravity relieves it of the lifeless skin of the erstwhile plump fruit.

The juice runs into vats, where it is concentrated by vacuum evaporation, until it is a thickish fluid. This is poured into five-gallon pails, and goes into a cold room with a temperature of 20 degrees Fahrenheit. There it is stored until a ship arrives at Stann Creek to take it to Tampa in Florida where further processing takes place. From there it goes by big trailer trucks to Canada. The concentrate is not used neat, as it is too strong for human consumption; it is diluted with juice from other sources to maintain a standard product.

The machinery of this plant is of American manufacture, and all the materials needed, such as pails, come from the United States. When I was in British Honduras the manager was an American, trained in the Florida plantations, and the plantation manager was an Englishman; but the works superintendent was a Belizean, Mr. Alfredo Awe (pronounced Ah-way). It is significantly illustrative of the composition of the new nation of Belize that his father was a Lebanese and his mother a mestizo lady from the El Cayo District.

The other company in the Stann Creek District also extracts orange juice, putting it up in tins ready for drinking, but is not equipped to produce the more modern frozen concentrate. Throughout the Colony local orange juice from the can is a favourite drink, and this is the most convenient way of carrying refreshment on trips.

Exports are almost entirely to Canada and Britain. If the costs of production could be kept down and the labour shortage alleviated, there are reasonable prospects for expansion; but world markets are at present glutted with citrus, and there is little immediate prospect of improved world market prices.

10. A FEW HURRICANES

BRITISH Honduras lies inside the hurricane belt of the American tropics. It is exposed every autumn to the risk of an unpredictable visit of this phenomenon. Atmospheric disturbances form out in the Atlantic Ocean between 10 and 20 degrees north of the Equator. A mass of air rises, swirling anti-clockwise, and the mercury in the barometer drops several inches. Masses of water vapour, circulated in the clouds, discharge immense quantities of rain.

Hurricanes proceed westwards with a slightly northerly trend. They sweep along the Tropic of Cancer in the months from June to November, and 10 or more of them will beat against the American continent in a season. The meteorologists have hit on the whimsical trick of giving them girls' names in alphabetical order every year, the first of the season beginning with A, and the second with B, and so on. The most recent to affect British Honduras have been Janet in 1955 and Anna and Hattie in 1961. This means that in 1955 it was the 10th hurricane of that year, and in 1961 the first and eighth of the series. No year is a copy of another; a feature of hurricanes is that one may strike today, and another, just as bad, may strike next week. It is on record that in the year 1813 Belize City was visited by a hurricane on 1st August and another broke over the town on the 13th of the same month.

The annals of British Honduras record a hurricane – the first of which official notice was taken – on 2nd September, 1787. It struck the settlement at three o'clock in the morning, and destroyed every house except one. Many lives were lost; all the public records were destroyed, not for the last time. Twenty-six years later came the twin hurricanes of August 1813, but it is not recorded what damage was done. On 31st August, 1864, another hurricane struck Belize and caused severe damage, but how much was lost was not assessed. We can be sure that the flimsy wooden sheds of the settlement could not resist winds up to 200 miles an hour. The place had to be rebuilt. In 1893 a very severe storm was recorded in the southern parts of the Colony, but it was not technically a hurricane; it passed to the south of the capital, doing great damage to crops and forests, but causing no loss of life.

In 1931 there happened the worst disaster that has ever scourged British Honduras. On 10th September a hurricane passed directly over the central part of the Colony. It happened on the anniversary of the Battle of St. George's Cay, the holiday celebrated every year by Belizeans as National Day. Meteorological science had not reached the efficiency that it displays today. Weather forecasting was in its infancy, and Watson-Watt had yet to bounce radio waves off thunderstorms to invent radar. Warnings of the approaching storm reached Belize by cable; but the path of the hurricane was forecast south of the city. Some vagary of Fate made it change course over the Caribbean Sea. It struck Belize City with all its force, the centre of the storm passing over the Capital. The maximum force was felt between the hours of two and six in the afternoon: but the winds, raging up to 150 miles an hour, were not the cause of the worst damage or the loss of life.

When a hurricane passes over the surface of the sea the wind raises a ridge of water, and wherever it strikes the coast the effect is that of an unnaturally high tide. It is not a tidal wave, for it occurs only at the centre of the storm; but it is enough.

On 8th September, 1931, the storm was reported moving westwards 150 miles south of Jamaica. On the ninth it was located 105 miles south west of Kingston, but was not regarded as potentially dangerous. At that time Belize City was preparing to celebrate National Day. In the evening there was a gorgeous display of fireworks from the point of Fort George, providing a rare sight for spectators on the south bank. The next day dawned with drizzle and cloud. The city was decorated in gala style with flags and bunting in the streets, and mothers were busy getting boys and girls ready for the march in the processions.

At nine o'clock in the morning the developing hurricane was 50 miles north of the port of Tela in Honduras, out in the Caribbean Sea. It was expected to beat against the mountains to the south, but the wind gauge in Belize City began to record gusts of 50 miles an hour, and the rain came down harder, dampening the decorations but not the enthusiasm of the people.

At 9.30 a.m. the wind was blowing steadily at 36 miles an hour. At 12.30 p.m. it was roaring at 48 miles an hour, and at 1.15 p.m. reached 60 miles an hour. The gale grew fiercer every minute. By 2.15 p.m. the gauge registered 72 miles an hour; at 2.30 p.m. 96 miles an hour and at 2.35 p.m. 120 miles an hour. The apparatus was designed to record only up to 125 miles an hour, but it managed to indicate 132 at 3.30 p.m. before collapsing under the strain.

Houses were blown out to sea with all their contents, including people, who were never seen again. The Jesuit college collapsed, and many of the schoolmasters were crushed to death. Children running home from the abandoned parades were blown into the river. At 3.40 p.m. there was a lull, as the eye of the hurricane passed slightly to the south. The wind dropped for a short space. Many people who thought that the worst was over ventured into the streets to enquire about relatives and friends. This confidence betrayed them into greater danger, for the hub of the storm quickly passed. The winds of the circumference rose again in all their fury. But what made it so deadly in effect was the arrival of the bulge of water raised on the surface of the sea by the pressure of the winds. Since it was a cyclone, the wind rose from a different quarter, the south-west, and brought a flood 15 feet deep. This lasted until 6 o'clock, when the wind began to abate and the water to recede. Meanwhile, large waves continuously washed

Fishing boat in mangrove swamp. Collecting sprats for bait.

over Belize City, as the sea rushed inland and covered the marshes at the back. It all happened so rapidly that many people in the streets were unable to reach the safety of buildings above the waves. They were swept out to sea. Many buildings, already weakened by the wind and rain, could not resist the attack and collapsed into the flood.

Then came the night as black as pitch under an overcast sky; not until next morning could the survivors measure the extent of the damage. The place was a shambles; 2,000 people were dead or missing. Not all the buildings collapsed, but stocks of food and goods were ruined, and the water system was out of action. Official calculation of the loss was $5,000,000. Many events in British Honduras are celebrated in ballads; one was soon composed in memory of the hurricane in 1931. The first verse goes:

'The tenth day of September
So dreadful to remember,
The Hurricane did strike Belize, Honduras
    on the Main.
By God it was ordained,
He sent that Hurricane
That struck Belize, Honduras on the Main.'

Other stanzas describe the dying children and their mothers' cries, and the 'terrible *bleatings* of the wind'.

This hurricane caused a definite turn in the political history of British Honduras, for recuperation was impossible without aid from the British Government.

Eleven years later, on 5th November, 1942, a little hurricane formed off the island of Puerto Rico, and travelled strangely, towards the Bahama Islands. By 6th November, with a wind recorded at 60 miles an hour, it swerved south-west towards the coast of British Honduras. Sunday 8th November dawned in Belize City with overcast skies and intermittent rain. By midday the winds had increased, and at four o'clock the gauge was registering over 50 miles an hour. Sheets of corrugated iron blown off the roofs were a danger to people in the streets. The sea rose about two feet over the high tide level, but no real inundation took place. The centre of the hurricane crossed the Colony to the north with gusts reaching 80 miles an hour. The towns of Corozal, Sarteneja, and others near the Mexican border were badly hit.

The worst damage, however, occurred on the islands and cays. Caye Corker was cut in two and many buildings in San Pedro village on Ambergris Cay were swept out to sea and completely vanished. Three out of every four coconut trees were blown over. Fishermen out at sea disappeared. The rise in the sea level caused most of the islands and cays to become mere shoals.

The damage was estimated at $4,000,000. The loss of life – nine dead – was remarkably low. The inhabitants of the cays had warning enough to cross over to the mainland.

On 28th September, 1955, Hurricane Janet was the first of the named hurricanes to affect British Honduras. It struck the same area that her elder sister had whipped in 1942. Janet was born in the Atlantic Ocean to the south of the West Indies, and caused a great deal of damage in the Windward Islands and Barbados before crossing the Caribbean Sea. Belize City escaped the worst of the storm, receiving some damage but no loss of life. The little town of Corozal took the full force of the blow and was completely destroyed. This place, the most northerly in British Honduras, was famous for its thatched houses, plastered inside and out with white marl which, from a distance at sea, gave the little town a splendid appearance. The houses were thatched with 'bay leaves', which lasted upwards of 30 years before needing to be replaced. They could not withstand the high winds of a hurricane. The churches of wood and brick stood up no better and collapsed.

It is significant that after these major disasters, new ideas and plans come forward, and the money is found to implement them. After Janet's visit, Corozal Town was rebuilt with government aid. An immediate grant of £10,000 was announced by Mr. Alan Lennox-Boyd, then Secretary of State for the Colonies, and a reconstruction and rehabilitation programme got under way. Corozal Town arose anew. The government built effectively and aided the construction of churches. For private houses a system of aided 'self-help' was devised, and has been most successful. The town was rebuilt on a modern town plan and was handed over to the Town Board in 1960. This method allowed the government to effect its great programme of general reconstruction.

Twelve persons died during this hurricane in one small town, and 15 communities were destroyed.

Late in the month of October 1961, a hurricane was seen in formation 50 miles east of Cape Gracias a Dios in the Republic of Honduras. It was the eighth in the series of that year and the name of Hattie was chosen to distinguish it. On 29th October it was moving northwards and seemed headed directly for the western end of Cuba. The anticipated direction was to the north-west, meaning that it would drift into the peninsula of Yucatán. The weather bureau in Miami sent warnings to all parts that might be affected, and Radio Belize relayed these warnings to the people of Belize. It was expected that only heavy rains and strong winds would be felt, and that the centre of the hurricane would pass well to the north. The Information Office in Belize displayed a chart with an arrow indicating the track of the storm, and the authorities began taking emergency measures in order to be prepared.

In the morning of 30th October the course of Hurricane Hattie was seen to be veering south. The storm was taking a south-westerly path, not north-west as had seemed probable earlier. Evacuation of Belize City was immediately begun. All those who had cars loaded them up with their families and most prized possessions and wended their way inland to the higher ground, even as far as San Ignacio, 72 miles west of Belize City. They were wise to do so. Distributors of cars and lorries filled the tanks of new vehicles with petrol and moved with them. This was providential, for after the hurricane had passed, the Army was able to requisition six new Land-Rovers, which were invaluable in the circumstances.

Those who had no motor transport flocked to the public buildings in Belize City as they were judged to be the stoutest and safest refuges. There seemed to be plenty of time, but Hattie had a surprise in store. The radio station gave periodic announcements of the progress of the hurricane, and at 12.55 a.m. on the 31st, advised that the next bulletin would be broadcast at four o'clock. At one o'clock the electricity supply failed and the radio station fell silent.

Winds of 150 miles an hour with gusts up to 200 miles an hour lashed the town from one o'clock onwards. The fury lasted eight or nine hours until the middle of the morning of 31st October; the sea rose 15 feet above the normal high tide level as the centre passed over the district of Stann Creek, 30 miles south of Belize City. Since hurricanes are cyclonic, blowing anti-clockwise round the eye, a phenomenon is the rapid change in direction of the wind. It blew at first from the west-south-west and this was quite visible in later weeks. Coming into Belize airport in February 1962 one could see from the windows of the aircraft that the trees blown over lay with their tips pointing north-east. Thousands of trunks lay aligned in the same direction. Then the wind had shifted, and blew from north-by-east, and finally it blew itself out from the east, as the rim of the cyclone drew away.

Many survivors had curious escape stories to tell. Fort George Hotel, of modern construction, was fairly secure against the gale, only the windows could be damaged. But when the inevitable ridge of water reached the coast of British Honduras, the sea overflowed the sea wall in front of the hotel, and covered the road. It invaded the garden, racing inwards along the street into the City. Soon it was over the front steps of the hotel, and the vestibule was awash. The guests took refuge on the second and third floors, and watched fascinated while the sea covered the reception desk. One American traveller, who had been given a downstairs room, climbed on to a table, expecting the flood to subside before long. When the table began to float around the room, he decided he had better seek a safer place. But he found the door was stuck, and he was imprisoned with the water rising around him. The door was jammed either by the force of the sea beating against it, or some debris had blocked the exit. Desperately he tried to break it down and could not. The water was around his neck before he finally managed to force a way out and reach the upper floors.

The loss of life was found to be 262 men, women and children. Of these the majority had been drowned by the rising sea water, as waves five feet high raced across Belize. A resident of one of the better houses in the Fort George area described it as like being in a boat. The waves travelled over the city as though there had never been land. That the loss of life was not greater was due to the timely warnings and the evacuation of the city. The losses occurred because of the changed direction of Hattie, which had been forecast to strike north of the capital city.

The devastation was of a kind an earthquake could not have surpassed. Indeed, some people were convinced that an earthquake did occur during the height of the storm. But any signs of shifted levels, cracks in the soil and other seismic phenomena can well be explained by the saturation of the subsoil, and the settling of dried-out sections. Worst of all was the mud – 12 inches deep. It was black when wet, and dried to a greyish crust and was composed of decayed organic matter. The stench it gave off in the heat of a tropical sun was overpowering. Even three months later, in February 1962, mud was a conspicuous feature of the streets and gardens of Belize City. The floor of the bay must have flowed on to the city.

Most of the trees were down but some survived, shorn of all leaves. Even the African palms with their tufts 20 feet long were reduced to stumps. Three months later they began to put forth new shoots. Outside the city coconut palms were overthrown by hundreds; not 10 per cent of the trees in a plantation near the airport had survived. Yet in the garden of the Hotel Fort George some delicate plants bowed to the storm and lifted their heads when it had gone; what was more, they survived the poisoning of the soil by the salt of the sea and the emanations of the mud. An engaging feature of Belize City before Hattie had been the crabs that burrowed in the gardens, in building sites or the edges of the roads. They would scuttle to shelter if one approached too near, but if one stood still and waited, they would peek out again in a few minutes. Their burrows were everywhere, running diagonally into the sandy earth. After the hurricane they were entombed in mud; it took months before they could find their way back into the city. Even today they are not as plentiful as they used to be.

Belize City was not the worst sufferer. Stann Creek Town was completely blown away, and the village of Mullins River disappeared as well. In Stann Creek some wooden houses, torn off their pillars by the force of the storm, were turned upside down and carried across the site of the town. Historic St. George's Cay was cut into three islets, and all the 30 houses that had been built on the island in modern times were washed away. The hurricane did not succeed in washing away St. George's Cay altogether, but other smaller cays disappeared for ever.

The enormous force of a hurricane wind is illustrated by the fact that half Government House was completely lost; its steel safe was recovered some hundreds of yards away in a swamp.

The first reports to reach the outside world said that Belize City had been totally destroyed; but this was an exaggeration. There was indeed much damage, as the photographs taken on the morning after the storm showed. Many of the humbler buildings were damaged and some of the principal structures, too; but 50 per cent of them stood up. There were gaps in the roofs, where the corrugated iron sheets – Belize's only roofing material – were gone. The market by the river was completely unroofed, as it had open sides, so the gusts of wind could get underneath and tear the sheets off. These roofs had been painted red with water-proofing material, and when they had been repaired, the patches of new zinc, recorded the extent of the damage. From the evidence it was seen that no house had not suffered some damage, and the average area of new roofing was about 30 per cent on all buildings.

Many streets were blocked with debris, fallen trees, poles and large masses of loose boards, from disintegrated buildings. But boards are not difficult to remove and can often be used again. Many humbler buildings leaned over as the pillars had collapsed under them. It was not too difficult a task to put up new pillars and haul the wooden structure back into place. Broken windows abounded, as any unprotected pane went early in the gale, and the wire mesh to exclude mosquitoes, without which life in Belize City would be torture, was torn and broken. Three months after the hurricane, Belize City looked almost normal. There were sections where electric light poles leaned drunkenly, many damaged houses were unoccupied, and some were completely down. Reconstruction was in full swing; the sound of hammering nails into wood was perpetual.

Vast destruction was inflicted upon the citrus plantations, which lay in the path of the centre of the storm. Trees were stripped of their leaves; the fruit was shaken off the branches until the entire year's crop was almost lost. In the forests of the interior, the taller trees most exposed to the gales were blown down by thousands. Some of the timber could be salvaged by logging operations, but many square miles were encumbered with a tangled mass of trunks and branches which made harvesting impossible. After the rainy season ended and the woods dried out in January, forest fires were inevitable; large areas were reduced to ashes, smouldering for many weeks. The houses in Belize City, the stocks of merchants' goods and the fruit crops of the processers were mostly insured against hurricane damage, but the forest products were a dead loss to the Colony.

Before help could reach the suffering city many people were

destitute, with no food, clothes or places to sleep. There was no drinking water, and all the goods in the shops had been under water for a whole night. Some became desperate, and looting began. At first it was merely hungry and thirsty people looking for food; but soon it got out of hand; looters were breaking and entering to steal anything of value. The local authorities were unable to control the situation and they called for help from the British Army. Six Britannias of RAF Transport Command flew in urgently needed troops and stores. As the airport was partially out of action six Coastal Command Shackletons and two Transport Command Hastings were sent to operate locally between Jamaica and British Honduras. Food distribution centres were speedily set up and typhoid inoculations were given to prevent epidemics. Military patrols circulated through the damaged town. One man was shot. He and two others were found breaking into a warehouse when the soldiers arrived. The intruders were challenged and ran off; one was shot in the leg. The other continued to run, and was brought down by a bullet that ended his life on the spot. There was no more looting after that.

Not all the loss resulted from looting. It is related that two merchants were surveying their soaked establishments after the hurricane; one was gloomy and the other was happy. The jubilant one explained to his neighbour that all his stock which was not ruined and which was portable had been carried off before he could arrive. He was cleaned out. The other had made a provisional calculation that he had lost at least 50 per cent of his inventory, and what was left had seriously deteriorated. 'Well,' said the first shopkeeper, 'I was fully insured against fire, flood, hurricane, riot and civil commotion. I can recover the loss and stock up afresh in a few months with entirely new goods, modern styles, and all that.'

The other stared aghast at the prospect. Then he had a bright idea. He also was insured against hurricane, riot and civil commotion. He threw open his doors and invited the hungry inside. 'Boys', he said jovially, 'everyone of you steal what he can lay his hands on. Take what you find, it's yours!' When the last shelf was bare he sighed with relief. One hundred per cent recovery in cash, and restocking with new goods – he could meet his competitor on an equal footing.

The insurance compensation received by merchants and companies operating in British Honduras for damage consequent on Hurricane Hattie amounted to £7,000,000. Not all of this was paid into banks in Belize City, as the foreign owned companies maintain bank accounts in London, New York and Jamaica. But the figures of bank deposits in the Royal Bank of Canada and Barclays Bank in Belize are eloquent. Private bank deposits at 31st December, 1960, were $BH7,077,000. On 31st December, 1961, two months after the hurricane, they reached $BH16,139,000 and $BH9,000,000 came into the hands of the merchants in Belize City from hurricane insurance payments. This is equivalent to £2,250,000. In September 1962, when restocking was in full swing, and the merchants and importers could have been expected to have used their money to buy goods, the deposits were still over $BH12,000,000.

The bank managers were delighted. Slow payers of overdrafts and overdue credit facilities paid off their outstanding debts. The bank loan figures tell the same tale as the deposits:

Bank loans in December 1960 were $BH6,100,000; in December 1961 $BH4,488,000, and in September 1962 $BH4,894,000.

A bank manager commented on the fact that some merchants in Belize City had never had so much money in their lives before; the feel of it was so pleasant that they applied for loans to restock, instead of using their own cash, despite the interest charges. Most of this insurance money came from London, although some was from New York.

In March 1962 stocks of goods in the shops were about 45 per cent of pre-hurricane size, and by September the recovery was about 75 per cent or 80 per cent. By Christmas 1962 the situation was normal.

There was some loss of employment at first; shopkeepers with no merchandise laid off assistants; but this was compensated for by the demand for labour to clear up and repair. There was at first an acute shortage of building materials and hardware, nails being essential and required in quantities far beyond the normal demand. Locks, hasps, hinges and all the thousand and one items that a wooden house needs, had to be imported, as the sea water had corroded the recovered items. The demand for carpenters and joiners outran the local supply. Wages rose, money circulated and came back into the tills of the shopkeepers of Belize City.

A year after Hattie life in Belize City had resumed its normal cheerfulness and would continue until the next hurricane strikes.

No account of Hurricane Hattie in British Honduras would be complete without mention of the prompt help received from the outside world. The British Government had given for Hurricane Janet's damage some £850,000 in former years. Between 1962 and 1966 no less than £3,000,000 were made available in Colonial Development and Welfare grants, loans and other aid. This enabled rapid reconstruction to take place. Immediately after the hurricane the other Central American countries sent medicines and food, and the United States of America sent an aircraft carrier with a squadron of helicopters, with 95 doctors, who made 29,000 inoculations against typhoid fever in one week. This figure alone will serve to give an idea of the international succour accorded to the territory.

11. TRADE AND FINANCE

DURING the first century and a half of their existence the British settlements in the Bay of Honduras depended on the logging industry, which was the only reason for their existence. Logwood was far more important than mahogany, and other woods were almost completely ignored. Some rosewood and other precious lumbers were obtained; but the high prices paid by the dyers of the seventeenth and eighteenth centuries made it far more profitable to specialize in logwood, with the result that the stands were exhausted. A logwood tree is a rarity now.

Unfortunately no statistics of the amounts cut are preserved, and we have absolutely no basis on which to figure the income. No calculation was made of the Belize trade, until Mr. Thompson was sent by the British Government in 1824 to establish relations with the newly founded Federated Republic of Central America. That gentleman stayed in Belize on his way there and on his return, and brought back some interesting figures of the entrepôt trade. At that time Jamaica was supplying £495,000 and Belize £1,650,000 worth of goods every year to Central America, through the ports of Trujillo and Omoa on the north coast of Honduras, and by scow through the swamps to Izabal, up the river of the same name in Guatemala. Central American exports were respectively: Jamaica £450,000 and Belize £1,700,000. From what is now British Honduras there was therefore an export of produce worth £50,000 per annum less than the value of goods received. The balance in favour of Central America was greater, for Mr. Thompson included in his figures the cost of freight to Izabal, which was at $2 per package. This charge was absorbed by the merchants in Belize, and amounted to £150,000 yearly, making the balance in favour of Central America about £200,000 or about a million Spanish dollars. (The very few accounts that have survived are all expressed in silver at five pesos to the pound sterling.)

To obtain the million pesos the merchants of Belize exported logwood and mahogany to Britain, and created a continual flow of money westwards. The phenomenon was not unnoticed by the rulers of Central America, both at federal and state level, and explains largely the favourable atmosphere for Consul Chatfield's manoeuvres in subsequent years. Central America had always been poor, so much so that the Spanish Colonial Government in Mexico during the monarchy had to subsidize the Captaincy General at Guatemala City with 100,000 silver dollars yearly. The taxes collected never could meet the public outlay. Far from despoiling the Spaniards in Central America, the Baymen were providing them with urgently needed foreign exchange.

The goods bought from Central America by Belize were indigo, cochineal, cacao, balsam and cotton, and to a lesser degree, hides and tobacco. There was even some coffee, although coffee was not the predominant crop that it became in later times. The English goods were textiles and hardware. The elegant uniforms which the presidents and generals wore for their portraits were of English cloth; President Morazán of the Federal Republic imported through Mr. Marshall Bennett of Belize a noble brass bedstead and two lamps, which must have delighted Mrs. Morazán as prestige symbols.

The entrepôt trade did not last many years. For a generation it prospered, and then towards the middle of the century the development of California caused a shift of the trade routes. Belize dropped behind. Bigger ships brought European goods direct to the mainland. In 1853, when the next statistical indication is available, Belize merchants were petitioning the Admiralty to establish better communications with the mother country, claiming that their yearly imports from Britain were £500,000, which is less than one-third of the figure 30 years before.

By 1879 the exports to Central America from Belize were down to only $82,000 consisting of rum and sugar only; and Belize drew from Central America, almost all from Spanish Honduras, foodstuffs, including meat and fruit, to the extent of $96,000. Forty-two years later, in 1921, exports had almost vanished at $12,000, but imports were up to $177,000. Trade was almost extinct, but whatever there was, created invariably a trade balance favourable to Central America.

Meanwhile, the nature of trade had changed. The introduction of synthetic dyes ruined the logwood trade, as better colouring matter could be obtained from coal tar far more cheaply than by processing bulky tree trunks. The lumber trade became confined to mahogany and 'cedar'. Pine began to be exported to the United States of America.

In the past centuries we read of many independent lumbermen in British Honduras, who continually quarrelled among themselves, and required the wisdom of Admiral Burnaby to keep them from each other's throats. As years went by the natural development of smallholdings into larger units took place. The better organized dealers with greater capital gradually ousted or absorbed their smaller and weaker brethren, until in our day only one large firm exports nearly all the lumber from British Honduras. Some lesser dealers do purchase and saw logs, but the Belize Estate and Produce Company Limited exports over nine-tenths.

This firm was acquired in 1947 by J. Gliksten and Sons Limited, of London. It owns 872,412 acres in British Honduras, all preserved as forest.

After three centuries of absolute sway King Lumber fell from his throne. Now both sugar and citrus surpass lumber. To illustrate this trend we can scrutinize the statistics for 1965, when out of total domestic exports of $15,217,000, lumber accounted for only $2,065,000 or 14 per cent, while citrus amounted to $3,824,000 or 25 per cent and sugar was on top with $5,030,000 or some 33 per cent.

How these competitors of the timber trade have flourished in recent years is demonstrated by the statistics of exports. Citrus fruit and products, such as tinned orange juice and concentrates, have grown yearly. Export figures were:

1950	$BH 543,000	1962	$BH1,410,000
1955	$BH 924,000	1963	$BH3,798,000
1959	$BH1,792,000	1964	$BH4,684,000
1961	$BH3,479,000	1965	$BH3,824,000

The loss of crop by Hurricane Hattie is graphically shown by the drop in 1962, but recovery was made the following year; and in any case, the loss was largely covered by insurance.

Sugar production has been even more spectacular. Production in 1963 was 25,000 tons. In 1964 it rose to 30,000 tons and to 35,000 tons in 1965. In 1967 production was 60,000 tons, following the opening of a new sugar refinery, and would have been higher still but for the low world prices. Production could reach 100,000 tons by 1970 if market outlets could be found. Exports have been worth:

1959	$BH2,312,000	1963	$BH5,229,000
1960	$BH2,108,000	1964	$BH5,621,000
1961	$BH4,053,000	1965	$BH5,030,000
1962	$BH3,928,000		

The financial situation of the colony has benefited immensely from these industries. The sugar crop is guaranteed a market in Britain for 35,000 tons a year for the period 1966–68, of which 20,500 tons is sold at the negotiated price amounting to about £47 a ton (compared with a current free market price of about £20 a ton) and the balance at world price plus Commonwealth preference, i.e. about £23 a ton in 1967. It also has a US quota of 10,000 tons a year for the period 1966–71. Thus about a half of current production is subject to the vagaries of world price.

In 1965 four principal items – lumber, citrus, sugar and resin – accounted for nearly 90 per cent of the domestic trade of British Honduras. Surprisingly, of the miscellaneous items that make up the 10 per cent remainder, shirts manufactured in Belize represent the major item, being $BH410,000 that year, or some 4 per cent of the domestic exports. The reason for this is that an enterprising firm of shirt manufacturers in the United States of America sends the cloth, and receives back the finished article. This is made possible because the labour cost is much lower, and the workmanship not inferior. British Honduras produces few consumer goods, as the market is too small to make much specialized manufacture possible.

Consequently, the importers are a prominent group in Belize, and even quite small businesses will bring their stocks in direct,

instead of purchasing from the wholesalers. There are about 150
importers and an analysis of their names is very revealing:

	No.	%
International companies	6	4
British surnames	41	27
Other European names	14	9
Creoles	15	10
Chinese	21	14
Syrian, Arab and other Near Eastern	20	14
Mestizos or Mexicans	33	22
TOTALS	150	100

The first group comprises the lumber, sugar and citrus
growers. They import supplies for their own consumption, such
as machinery and spare parts; but two of them, the Belize Estate
and Produce Company and the British Honduras Distributers
Ltd., import vehicles and machinery for general purposes, and
maintain showrooms in Belize City. Of the second group, with
British surnames, a few are American citizens of white race. The
majority are predominantly of European extraction, but not all.
The same remarks can be applied to the non-British surnames.
The holders are mostly white, and all are citizens of British
Honduras. The distinction is academic, and of no practical
significance. The fourth group, Creoles, is composed entirely of
shopkeepers with grocery stores and small general businesses;
they import part of their goods direct. These importers are not
rich men, and their aggregate capital does not equal that of a
single one of the bigger importers. This is a pity, for one would
like to see them participating in the trade of British Honduras
to a larger and more representative extent.

There is hardly a Chinese in British Honduras who is not a
shopkeeper or merchant; but not all of them are direct importers, and the total number of Chinese in the colony is more than
the twenty-one shown. With their families they must number
nearly 200.

The Near Eastern immigrants are mostly Lebanese, but there
are some Arabs from Bethlehem. They, too, are all traders, but
some are only shopkeepers who do not import for themselves,

or whose direct imports are made under the name of another of their group, for that is quite a common practice among this class. In contrast with the Chinese, they frequently branch out into activities other than shopkeeping, and become farmers, or industrialists. A prominent member of the Syrian colony, for example, trades in chicle gum export, sugar cane planting and dairy farming, as well as having founded two shops. This gentleman has accumulated a fortune, and not by rapacity. He is generous and has made many donations to his adopted country.

Perhaps the most interesting group is the last, that of persons with Spanish surnames. Most of them are descendants of the Mexicans who, in the nineteenth century, took refuge in British Honduras when the Mayan Indians of Yucatán were asserting their claims to self-determination. They have been residents of British Honduras for five or six generations, settled in the northern and western parts of the territory. Also there is a strong element of Mexicans of recent immigration, some of whom retain their Mexican nationality, although many have adopted British citizenship. They are very keen traders. Some have quite a lot of capital, and have invested their surpluses in agricultural land. They do not confine themselves to commerce, but have dairy produce, freighting, and other interests, and take part in the planting of sugar cane on rented land in the northern districts. In fact, many of the Mexicans were first attracted to British Honduras by the good prospects of sugar cane cultivation, and by the guaranteed price for the cane delivered to the mill at Corozal; from there they have branched out into trade. These activities contribute to their growing importance in the economic life of British Honduras. The original planting provided money to start in business; and the profits of trade were reinvested in more planting, in an unending chain. They accumulate capital more rapidly than any other of the groups, except perhaps the Near Eastern section.

Imports usually exceed exports. This adverse balance of trade (£4.8 million in 1966) is only made possible in British Honduras because the influx of funds from overseas has been sufficient to finance it. The inflow has taken the form of cash assistance from the British Government for hurricane rehabilitation, budget support, development aid and a considerable amount of private capital mainly in connection with investment in the citrus and sugar industries.

For a number of years British Honduras has had difficulty in balancing its budget. The following table shows expenditure and revenue from 1962 to 1967; as can be seen the hurricane had a drastic effect on the budget figures for 1963:

	1962	**1963**	**$BH'000** **1964**	**1965**	**1966**	**1967** (*Est.*)
Current Revenue	9,335	9,108	10,492	10,954	10,610	11,667
Current Expenditure	8,427	9,288	8,933	9,430	10,951	11,964
Surplus (+) or deficit (−)	+908	−180	+1,559	+1,524	−341	−297
Capital Expenditure	3,531	7,931	3,744	4,078	3,790	7,025
Total Deficit	−2,623	−8,111	−2,185	−2,554	−4,131	−7,322

The deficits have been financed (almost entirely by the British Government) in the following ways:

	1962	**1963**	**$BH'000** **1964**	**1965**	**1966** (*Est.*)
Colonial Development and Welfare grants	909	1,576	1,485	1,537	812
Grants in aid	2,002	946	694	500	300
External loans and grants	118	3,917	2,183	519	2010
Changes in British Honduras Treasury balances (−=increase)	−406	+1,672	−2,177	−2	+171

In short to enable the territory to balance its budget, maintain its development expenditure and make good the damage done by the hurricane, Britain has made available nearly $BH20 million (£5 million) up to 1966.

A lady journalist from up north once demanded of a Governor of British Honduras: 'Just when are you Britishers going to give the Belizeans their freedom?' That functionary replied: 'Madam, as soon as we can, without allowing them to go broke'.

However, the prospect is not so bleak as at first appears.

Recently local revenue has been increasing at a higher rate than budgetary expenditure and budgetary assistance has accordingly been decreasing as can be seen from the grant in aid figures on page 127. Payment of grant in aid ceased at the end of 1966 and the territory now makes some contribution to development expenditure, although the greater part of this will need to be financed from external sources for many years to come.

* * *

The British Honduras dollar is fixed at 4 to the £1 sterling or some $0.60 US currency.

* * *

'Why,' cried a USA citizen, when he proffered travellers' cheques and received a fistful of British Honduras notes, 'do they call them *dahlers* when they just ain't real *dahlers*?' During the early part of its history Belize used any currency that was available, and arguments over the relative rates of exchange were endless. In the eighteenth century British money from Jamaica was prevalent. In the nineteenth, the Spanish American pesos and reales, called dollars and rials in English, were dominant, owing to the needs of the entrepôt trade to conform with the monetary units of Central America. Then with the Californian gold rush and the increasing influence of the United States, American gold dollars circulated. The colony passed a decree in 1855 that made it obligatory to carry accounts in dollars and rials, but soon changed over to the decimal coinage of dollars and cents. The Spanish and the United States dollars were quoted at par. In 1887 the silver peso of Guatemalan mintage was declared the legal unit in the colony; but in 1894 this was changed to the United States dollar, and so remained, although the exchange rate was linked to the pound sterling.

Banking had been a private function in the colony, exercised by the leading merchants, until in the year 1904 the Bank of British Honduras was founded by a group of local financiers. This institution issued private notes which were expressed in dollars. They were linked by law to dollars and were equivalent in value. In 1912 this bank was bought by the Royal Bank of Canada, which took over the responsibility for the notes in circulation, and continued to issue bills until 1937. On 29th January of that year the Currency Commission was founded, and the function of providing currency for the Colony passed out of private hands. No central reserve bank was created; perhaps at that time such an institution was not required. The Canadian bank handed over sufficient assets to offset the liability of which it was relieved.

When the pound was devalued in September 1949 (and became equivalent to $2.80 compared with $4.03 previously), the British Honduras dollar was not devalued immediately. Apart from the fact that any alteration would have entailed special legislation, the close traditional economic relationship of the colony with the dollar area necessitated a very thorough examination of the case for altering the exchange value of its currency. In the event it was decided to devalue, and the rate was altered on 31st December, 1949, to $4 = £1 sterling. At the same time the direct link with the US dollar was ended and British Honduras adopted the sterling exchange system. As a result of the devaluation of sterling, the British Honduras dollar was devalued 14.3 per cent in November 1967.

The currency is in the form of bank notes of denominations of $1, $2, $5, $10, $20 and coin of 50, 25, 10, 5 and 1 cents, and from the proportions of the sundry values, it does not seem that there is much hoarding of large denominations as savings. This is in marked contrast to the Spanish American countries adjacent to British Honduras, such as Guatemala or El Salvador, where as much as 50 per cent of the high denominations never see the light. The annual amounts of notes in circulation in the colony since 1960 have been as follows:

1960	$BH2,189,000	1964	$BH3,232,000
1961	$BH2,983,000	1965	$BH3,522,000
1962	$BH2,847,000	1966	$BH3,730,000
1963	$BH3,048,000		

British Honduras has no independent monetary system and the Currency Commissioners do not control the volume of local currency. They are under a statutory obligation to issue local currency on demand against sterling lodged in London and to redeem it for sterling in London at a fixed rate. In the past colonial currency boards were required to maintain 100 per cent and sometimes 110 per cent currency backing in sterling, but since 1954 they have been able to invest a proportion of their currency funds in the securities of the Colony Government. This system ensures an adequate backing for the local currency and although it has certain disadvantages it prevents locally induced inflation.

When old notes are dirty, the banks withdraw them from circulation and receive equal amounts in new ones, which of course does not affect the situation at all. If the banks should have too much money on hand, which is doubtful as the continual growth of the population makes it very unlikely, they could hand the surplus notes to the Currency Commissioners in exchange for sterling.

12. THE CAYS AND THE REEF

TOURISM in our day bids fair to be the world's major industry. It is the biggest producer of foreign exchange for many countries, and the main source of livelihood for many places. British Honduras is gradually becoming a tourist attraction for people from the United States, as the possibilities of the Florida Keys have been practically exhausted and the delights of Cuba have cooled down to freezing point by political events.

Now that the scourges of malaria and yellow fever have been eliminated, the coast of Central America is ideal for tropical holidays. The climate is not too hot; every afternoon in Belize City the sea breeze starts up at three o'clock and makes the evenings pleasantly cool. Tourists began to arrive after the second world war and today provide the major part of the trade of the Fort George Hotel. Visitors from up north were the first to come, but excursions are now being organized from Mexico and Central American countries in increasing numbers. If the flow of visitors continues to increase, the accommodation available in Belize City will fall far short of the minimum necessary, and more hotels will have to be built. The Fort George is already booked solid at the peak of the season, and it has become very necessary to telegraph a reservation well in advance.

A pioneer in the tourist trade was Mr. Vic Barothy, who organized the fishing lodge on the Belize River by the airport. This is the cream of the trade, drawing to itself fishing enthusiasts by advertising in the sporting magazines. They are a strange breed of men, these fishermen, who spend a great deal of money on weird looking tackle, and even more on getting to odd parts of the oceans.

After them come the trailer gypsies, who drift down the road from Mérida in Yucatán, through Valladolid to Chetumal, and cross the Hondo River into British Honduras. In contrast with the fishermen, these newcomers spend as little as they can. They are often elderly couples on pensions, who would like to travel before they die, but who cannot afford to stay at the best hotels. Then come the army of excursionists who are decanted from chartered aeroplanes. They of course demand amusement, and although Belize City was at first unprepared to put itself out, the prospect of earning money by attending to their demands is producing a trade in souvenirs, lodgings and nightclubs.

The greatest tourist asset in the colony is the barrier reef and cays. There is nothing comparable to this feature in all the Americas, Europe and Asia combined. To find a similar reef one has to go to Australia, and even then the Great Barrier Reef of Queensland does not have the cays. They are unique.

The reef begins in the north by Ambergris Cay, which is separated from the Mexican territory by the shallow narrow channel of Bacalar Chico Cut. Although Ambergris Cay is technically an island, deer and ocelots can be found in its thickets and they must have come from the mainland forests. The Cay extends for about 21 miles from north to south and about five miles at its widest; it is broken up into sections by lagoons and inlets. To the west lies the channel between the cay and the mainland at Corozal Town; the origin of Ambergris Cay would seem to be the silt brought down by the Hondo River.

The report of the British Honduras Land Use Survey Team (1959) describes Ambergris Cay in the following terms: 'The connected chain of coral islands known collectively as Ambergris Cay (was) formed from the accumulation of coral fragments . . . first as a shoal patch. These shoals tend to build up in long lines parallel to the coast of the mainland. It is thought that their orientation may be connected with submarine geological strata rather than being entirely the work of sea currents'.

Stand on Ambergris Cay, and the first and only impression will be of sand, fine sand, wind-blown from the beach, forming a dune thinly grown with grass and bents. It reminded me of Dawlish Warren in Devonshire. The contrast inland is startling with swampy patches of black mud from decayed vegetation, and palm trees and bushes that make quite a dense forest. The western side of the cay faces the mainland at Corozal, with the estuary of the Hondo River in between. Like all coastal spits it grows by beach drift and is continually mutilated by storms.

A small aeroplane provides a service twice a week between

Belize City and Ambergris Cay, but the way by sea is pleasant. From a launch the coast looks low and flat. An irregular growth of coconut trees, palmetto and bushes fringe the white beach; the first signs of life will be found about five miles away at the southern tip at the village of San Pedro.

Here the people are mostly of Indian blood, but consider themselves to be mestizos; their language is Spanish, as is the name of the settlement. San Pedro looks picturesque from the sea, as the sun shines on white walls and red roofs; but ashore the glare from the walls can bother the eyes, and visitors are well advised to wear sunglasses.

A steep wind-blown beach of loose sand makes walking difficult. The straggling line of about 30 wooden houses makes no pretence at being on a street, which would be a luxury in a place with no wheeled vehicles at all. The local store, thanks to the wholesalers of Belize, is remarkably well stocked. After all, San Pedro does have some holiday visitors from the city, and week-end parties for bathing and fishing are becoming popular. Furnished lodgings are available in one or two of the recently built houses.

Sprat fishing with cast net. Rules and regulations have been established for the fishing industry.

As we got out of the skiff, leaving the launch about 100 yards from the beach, we were met by a very large policeman in a sun helmet.

'The village constable, gentlemen,' he greeted us. 'At your service. What can we do for you?'

He was a Carib from Punta Gorda at the southern extremity of British Honduras, near the Guatemala border. He seemed extraordinarily young. We went to the police station, consisting of a two-roomed cottage on stilts, with a cell of strong planks. The constable said that he experienced very little trouble; at week-ends he occasionally had to lock up some reveller, who had been indulging in 'chicha' – home-brewed malt from sugar cane juice and maize – to cool off until Monday morning.

San Pedro's own electric plant supplies power to the cold room of a fishermen's co-operative. They catch lobsters in the reef and gather conchs, which they export to the United States. Many a scallop in a seafood restaurant in Miami and New York started life as a conch in San Pedro. There was a heap of shark skins in the plant, waiting shipment to a tannery in the USA, which specializes in special polishing material, and the fins are sold for the Chinese delicacy, shark fin soup. The supply is limited, as only those sharks that get caught in the turtle nets are taken, and the total yearly catch is only about 150. The turtle is the hawk's bill; it goes into soup for aldermen's banquets, and the shell, in scales about six or eight inches across, is sent to Mexico to be made up into combs and jewellery.

The co-operative has about 50 members. It was organized by the government to provide better and more equitable marketing facilities than the former method of selling catches outright to a dealer from Belize City. It functions well and the fishermen get the maximum prices possible.

We decided to explore the place. Walking in the loose sand was so tedious that we descended to the water's edge where the going was better. The beach was of pale yellow sand, almost white, and seemed to be pulverized coral mixed with shell fragments. Innumerable seashells had been cast up from the reef. The tide at San Pedro rises and falls about two feet at the most, but 400 yards out to sea the line of never-ending foam showed where the breakers of the Caribbean shattered themselves on the coral. The reef does not protrude above the water, but makes it shallow enough for the combers to fall over in spray.

We went into the infirmary with its quiet, pleasant nurse. The two sick beds were unoccupied. The nurse, a Creole from Belize City, acts as midwife if necessary, and doses small children for the usual ailments. For accident cases needing surgery she calls up Belize City on the radio-telephone and a small plane can arrive within 20 minutes on the landing strip at the back of the village. Occasional epidemics of influenza break the monotony, but she confessed that it was an uneventful place. To amuse herself she had been collecting seashells from the beach below the clinic, and had a splendid display of the most beautiful specimens. Big glass floats from fishing nets, some of which have travelled from as far away as the coasts of Portugal, are sometimes cast up on the beach; she had gathered several of these to hang as ornaments in her room.

San Pedro was founded in 1849 by refugees from Bacalar in Quintana Roo and had then an 'Alcalde', in the Spanish style. This made the Mexican authorities claim it as part of Mexico in 1851; but the inhabitants protested, claiming that they were British subjects. There was quite a controversy over the matter: much deliberation took place between the foreign offices in Mexico and London. The matter was arranged amicably by the Treaty of Boundaries on 8th July, 1893, when Mexico fully recognized British sovereignty. There is no other settlement on all Ambergris Cay except a hamlet at the very northern tip, called Bacalar Chico from the home town of the original inhabitants. In front of it across the strait is the Mexican village of Xcalak, inhabited by Mayan Indians.

Eighteen miles south-east of San Pedro within the reef is Cay Caulker, or Corker. It is spelt both ways and both have the same pronunciation. Everyone on the island called it Cayo Icaco in Spanish. It is a sandy islet about three of four miles long and about a furlong wide, and it houses a fishing village of about four hundred people. They speak Creole and English, but I found it easier to communicate with them in Spanish, which is the language they speak among themselves. These people are Indians from Quintana Roo, handsome men, with stocky, robust bodies and ruddy complexions, quite distinct from the Mopan Maya of Succotz and the Kekchi of San Pedro Columbia in the Toledo District. Their ancestors came down from the mainland, the Peninsula of Yucatán, about two generations ago. I asked them if any of them spoke the Indian language still, and they pointed to an elderly man, who was the last of the tribe to use their ancestral tongue. They will lose their Spanish tongue before long, and become English speaking entirely. The fine, well-built elementary school on the island, teaches in English. So yet another linguistic relic will pass.

It was February when I was there and the fishermen were not fishing. They were lolling under coconut trees with a bottle of rum, but they were not drunk. I was offered a swig, but had to refuse. For conservation purposes the Government imposes an overall limit on the amount of lobsters to be caught each year, and apportions individual quotas to groups of fishermen. The closed season runs from 14th March to 14th July, the spawning season. A marine biologist provided by the United Nations studied the lobster industry and confirmed the need for conservation – not much to the taste of the fishermen, who would like to catch the lobsters that seem to abound in the sea and which would bring fine prices in the United States of America. The men we chatted with had completed their quotas.

The catch is marketed by a co-operative, which has been successful. The place shows every sign of prosperity. They have money in the bank, and have installed an electric light plant, and were talking about having proper sewage disposal to replace the pit latrines they have at present. The co-operative was formed under government patronage and supervision after Hurricane Hattie had demolished the lobster tail canning plant at Belize City. This plant was operated by a private company which bought the catch at rather low prices from disappointed fishermen. The price they now get by exporting their catch from their own refrigerator plant in Belize City is four times the amount received before the co-operative was established, and they are helped, it must be admitted, by the price increases for lobsters in the USA.

The alfresco meeting into which we intruded was discussing a business proposal. They had $10,000 in the bank, and since every man had his boat and his outboard motor, the money was not immediately needed by them. A merchant in Belize City had therefore suggested that they might lend him $3,000 on reasonable security. They seemed eminently capable of looking after their own affairs on Cayo Icaco.

One reaches the island from a little jetty on the west or leeward side, sheltered from the waves raised by the easterly breeze. The reef and its breakers, about half a mile out to sea, are clearly visible from the beach. The cay is nowhere more than 10 feet above sea level, but it is not entirely sand. Some soil has formed under the trees and the houses have mostly small gardens with papayas and other fruit trees. In the village I looked in vain for the 'icacos' or cocoplums that give the place its name. They are found only at the southern end of the island now. Coconut palms have been planted and have survived hurricanes, and there are 'guayabas', but they cannot be self sown and must have been brought there.

On Cay Caulker the lobster traps are made from Spanish cedar planks and ribs of cohune palm leaves. The trap, about four feet long, a foot wide and a foot deep, has a sliding trap door on the top. No bait is used. It is lowered into the water with stones, and for some reason known only to lobsters they creep inside and stay there until they are pulled up and lose their tails, which is fatal to a lobster. As the materials for the traps do not grow on the isle, the co-operative buys them in Belize City and ships them to the cay, but the traps are made entirely by the men themselves.

Another local industry is the carving of decoys for the turtles: A hawk's-bill turtle, head and all, is carved from a single piece of cedar. In the lagoon turtles think it is another turtle, come to pay a friendly call and are netted by the boatmen. As tourist curiosities they would probably sell well, although the size, a yard or so long, makes them inconvenient to carry.

Five miles south of Cay Caulker is Cay Chapel, smaller and recently uninhabited. The vegetation is not as varied as that of its neighbour, consisting of a wiry reed-like grass and mangroves with a few palms, which must have been planted. A house once stood there, but after Hurricane Hattie no sign of any construction remained. An American group has bought the isle and proposes to build a fishing lodge there.

Half-way back to Belize from Cay Caulker, leaving Cay Chapel on the port side is famous St. George's Cay. It is, or was, about two miles long, shaped like a letter 'L' which has fallen over backwards with its toe in the air. It is in the process of being washed away and redeposited by the currents and the wind. Hurricane Hattie cut it into three pieces, and changed the shoreline out of recognition. Perhaps in former centuries this islet was larger. It is said that the population in the eighteenth century, when the Spaniards from Yucatán made their famous raid, was as high as 400. It would be very difficult to house that number on the cay now; it is barely 50 yards wide. They told me that an old graveyard lies there. I could not find it; it is possible that the site is now under water.

About a dozen houses were built on the cay by wealthy merchants of Belize City for their week-ends and holidays. The largest is owned by a shoe manufacturer of Guatemala. Half of these pavilions, ruined by the hurricane, have been rebuilt. They glow with gay colours. Their fences have been nailed back into place and pines and coconuts have been planted in the sandy yards. The natural vegetation seems to be only mangroves and reed grass; when the pines and flowers were planted around the houses, seeds of the common weeds of Central America must have been brought in the earth from the mainland, and the weeds have established themselves. Despite the improvements and a more varied vegetation, the place is going down. The next hurricane may sweep it away for ever.

Twenty-five miles to the east of St. George's Cay are the Turneffe Islands, to which one goes through a gap in the reef. Through the light blue and green water of the lagoon the bottom is clearly visible, the depth in places being not more than a few fathoms. Outside the reef the colour of the water changes to deep Prussian blue and the depth drops from 50 to 500 feet. It was a January day when I went there. A strong north wind blew down from the United States, where blizzards swept the prairies at twenty degrees below zero. It was fresh enough on the sea to make one put on a jumper. The launch went southeastwards and high waves beat down from the north. The sky was cloudy, and when walls of water rose above one's head their colour was a semi-transparent glowing black, like volcanic obsidian. Sudden squalls can rise in this channel and small boats have been lost there. We threw out fishing lines. In a few minutes we had hooked a mackerel of about seven pounds. That was luck. We left the lures trailing behind the launch and caught nothing more until late afternoon, when an 18 lb. kingfish took the hook.

The crew of the launch said it was a bad day for fishing.

Belize City and the inshore cays had long since gone under the western horizon. In the middle of the channel we were alone and might have been in mid-Atlantic. It was awesome, but soon a line of tree tops showed over the horizon to the port bow, and the water began to get lighter again. The islands came into view. They are 40 miles long from north to south and 25 miles from east to west. We were heading for the extreme southern point, a spit of sand called Little Cay Bokel.

The water had now turned to a light china blue. I looked over the side of the launch and we were almost scraping the bottom as we entered a channel between the mangrove swamps. I could see no land under the trees, which grew in the water; but soon a few inches of sand appeared at the roots where a beach had formed. A pelican or two was the only sign of life. We passed through the channel in water as calm as a pond, then crossed a strait towards Little Cay Bokel. There was a red roof and some coconut palms – a sure sign of man's intervention. We anchored near a wooden jetty which ran 50 yards into the shallow water, and went ashore.

We found an acre or two of sand dune, grown over with tufts of coarse grass and surrounded on three sides by mangrove swamps. A dozen or so coconut trees must have been planted some 20 years ago; many more have been sown in the last two years. Their tufts of leaves poked out of the sand in two lines on either side of a paved path, just wide enough for one person. There is a good beach for bathing. Some mangrove seedlings have taken root, a warning that left alone they will make a forest of the beach in a few years.

The fishing lodge, or hotel, consists of a group of cabins on piles; the central building serves as a club house with dining room and a well-equipped kitchen. The cook was a mestizo from Benque Viejo del Carmen, and his helpers, the gardeners and the mechanics, were from Belize City. The four fishing guides there knew every nook and cranny where the big fishes lurk, and they take the guests out in the launches and skiffs. A place like that could do with 20 outboard motors, to be on the safe side; a capable mechanic was in charge of the motors and the lighting plant. He had a workshop by the jetty and had plenty to do.

One of the guests sauntered down to meet us, an American gentleman from Denver, Colorado.

'Only six hours by plane,' he said dreamily, 'but, boy, what a difference!'

Another guest was standing at the edge of the water with a fishing rod in his hands. 'I could fish all day,' he said, 'and I do just that.' He reeled in his line and produced at the end of it a baby barracuda, about eight inches long. He unhooked it and threw it back into the sea.

'Have you been fishing all this week?' I asked, amazed.

'Yep. Must have caught a hundred of them at least.'

'And what have you done with the fish?' There must have been other people fishing and they must have pulled in more fish, perhaps not a hundred each, but at least a dozen a day, and the total count was a lot more fish than I could imagine myself disposing of, with Belize only 40 miles away.

'Threw every one of them back.' he replied triumphantly.

'You want to know what I like about this place?' he enquired, as he cast the line into the water again.

A Carib dance of some religious significance. Troupes of these dancers and singers sometimes tour the towns.

'The fishing, the air, the sunlight, the exotic surroundings, the warmth,' I hazarded a few guesses.

'Hell, no!' he said. 'Not a telephone in the whole place. That's what I like about it.'

A stay of a week in a place like that would cost about $500 US currency. There must be dozens of similar sites that could be used as holiday resorts on the Turneffe Islands, where relaxation cannot be surpassed in the world.

The group consists of hundreds of islets and mangrove swamps, and supports some industries, such as sponge fishing and coconut plantations on the larger islands. It is a maze of channels and sandbanks, which only the local men can learn to know; the channels change direction with almost every storm. Strangely enough, although 25 miles of deep water separate the Turneffe group from the nearest cay and it is 40 miles to the mainland, some of the larger islets, such as Little Cay Bokel itself, have snakes of the boa constrictor kind, and racoons, in addition to rats and mice. How those animals and reptiles could have got there is a mystery, but there they are, along with the iguana lizards and the sea birds.

The cays stretch 130 miles along the coast of British Honduras in their hundreds. They are mostly temporary, formed by a shoal on the coral rock of the continental shelf, where a mangrove seedling may take root. A growth of vegetation in the shallow water accumulates sand around its roots; the sand builds up until it is permanently above the surface of the sea. Then it becomes a cay, until some change in the currents or a hurricane wipes it off the map. After Hurricane Hattie in 1961, well known places like Rendezvous Cay – where some Cambridge students stayed, when preparing their book, 'From the Cam to the Cays' – were washed away. Rendezvous Cay is today a shoal covered at high tide. Down in the south, opposite Punta Gorda, there are many cays with signs of Maya occupation, shown by the shards of ancient pottery in the soil of Wild Cane Cay, and it has been said that the cays may have been joined to the mainland at one time. That changes in sea level have taken place along this coast is apparent, but what seems more likely to have happened was a recent elevation of the land rather than a transgression of the sea. Perhaps Wild Cane Cay was a sacred spot for the Mayas, a kind of Island of the Blessed.

Those cays, shifting spots of sand, sparsely covered with coarse grass and bushes, are death traps in the hurricane season; the only source of fresh water comes from the rain, usually collected from the roof. Yet they exert a most powerful attraction. Once it has been felt, one can never escape the spell. A longing to go back possesses one – to stay there and let the world go by on its meaningless whirl. Perhaps that is the real reason for the presence of the fishermen, whose fishing is a mere excuse for escapism. One can understand why a successful American physician spends his holidays at Little Cay Bokel, throwing back into the sea the fish he pulled out of it.

13. MISCELLANEOUS REMARKS

IT is the declared intention of Her Majesty's Government that the Colony of British Honduras (to give it that designation for the last time) shall become independent. It will then be the State of Belize in Central America. Belize might naturally wish to join the Central American block, and to become a member of the ODECA, the Organization of Central American States, the pint-sized United Nations of that part of the world. Once the formula for a resolution of the dispute with Guatemala has been found, it is to be hoped that the other countries of Central America would welcome Belize as a sister republic.

The great advantage that Belize possesses is the good nature of her people. They are intelligent above the average, well behaved, industrious and healthy. Perhaps their best characteristics are their emotional maturity, their lack of complexes.

Most important to the Belizean is happiness around him; he knows that the worst enemy of happiness is envy of one's neighbour. Therefore he envies nobody, least of all speculators and the get-rich-quick fraternity. This does not mean that he does not appreciate a good standard of living, based on sound national finances and a healthy, growing economy. It is precisely this objective that engages so large a part of the energy of the government.

To co-ordinate the efforts of people who help themselves by helping their neighbours is a gigantic task. The Creole and the Carib, the mestizo and the Indian, are one in this ambition. All of them seem imbued with the spirit of Belizean nationality; they are willing to put the needs of the nation first. Of this spirit there are numerous examples, demonstrated in their daily tasks. Few people deny the essentially Christian basis of the impulse. When unselfishness is enthroned as a political principle, we can feel assured that the greatest good will come to the greatest number.

Belize is of course far from perfect. The issues on which personal ambitions ride have given birth to political parties; but even to the most discerning eye, the differences between them are not greater than those between Tweedledum and Tweedledee. The People's United Party supports Mr. George Price, who is 'our great leader'. The National Independence Party opposes Mr. Price, who is 'God's punishment on us for our sins', as an old lady in Belize once described the situation. Mr. Price is a man with a great natural talent for politics. He has been able very successfully to identify his country's interests with those of his party and his own interests.

George Cadle Price was born on 15th January, 1919, one of a family of three brothers and seven sisters, the progeny of William Cadle Price and his wife, Irene Escalante de Price. The family was strongly Catholic; after education in the Holy Redeemer School in Belize, young George studied for two years in St. Augustine Seminary in the State of Mississippi in the United States of America. His intention to become a priest was frustrated; but observers have noted a Jesuitical singleness of purpose, and a religious devotion to his goal, in everything that Mr. Price has done yet.

An early predilection for politics was soon manifested. George Price stood for election in 1943 to the Belize City Council and was defeated at the polls. He sought election again in 1947 and was successful, retaining his seat until he retired in 1965. He served as Mayor of the city of Belize for two terms.

In 1949 the British Honduras dollar was devalued and this measure caused, or was the excuse for, social discontent. A 'People's Committee', formed under the auspices of George Price, John Albert Smith, Leigh Richardson and Philip Goldson, changed itself into the People's United Party on 29th September, 1950. The first leader was Smith, who resigned in 1951, charging his associates with having received funds from Guatemala. Messrs. Richardson and Goldson went on trial for sedition, and in fact $500 were received from Guatemala to defray the expenses of their defence. After his release in 1954 Mr. Richardson became leader, and led the party to victory in the elections, which were the first under universal adult suffrage. In 1956 the party split; Messrs. Richardson and Goldson left the party and Mr. Price has been in unchallenged power since then. In 1957 the PUP won all nine seats in the Legislative Assembly.

All the discontented elements formed political parties of more or less momentary existence; they coalesced into a united oppo-

sition to Mr. Price from 1958 onwards as the National Independence Party. In 1961 it polled 24 per cent of the votes, but did
not win a seat in the Legislative Assembly. In 1965 it polled 39
per cent of the votes and won two seats; and in the municipal
elections of 1966 won three of the seven town boards. With two
Assemblymen the party cannot be ignored, and it is treated as an
official opposition on the political stage.

The duty of an Opposition, to oppose, is thoroughly carried
out by the NIP, which accuses Mr. Price of having tried to sell
Belize, 'lock, stock and barrel' to Guatemala. One of their
charges is based on his having been expelled from the Executive
Council in 1957 on his return from a conference in London to
discuss constitutional advance, when he and a fellow member
from Belize had secret talks with the Guatemalan Minister in
London, Sr. Granados. They explained that they had merely
listened to some proposals put forward by the Guatemalan
Minister. Perhaps Mr. Price was applying some leverage for his
own ends as well.

This remarkable man commands a good majority of votes in
elections that we can be sure have been free and unhindered, and
which truly reflected the will of the people of Belize. He is not
eternal, and will either fall from power, or be removed by the
passage of years; but it is only fair to say that while he has been in
office Mr. Price has not abused his power.

Independence will present economic and financial problems
which must be firmly taken in hand. What of the currency issue?
The present currency arrangements are outlined on page 129.
When the territory is no longer a colony it will no doubt set up its
own central bank and control its own issue of currency. Where
will the currency find its backing – London, the sterling area, or
in New York, the dollar area? Will inclusion in the dollar area be
a concomitant of joining the Organization of Central American States? Will retention in the sterling area mean exclusion
from ODECA, and continued political isolation from the neutral
hinterland of Belize? These are practical points that will have
to be thrashed out in long, and probably acrimonious,
debates.

Another problem which has to be tackled is that of land. On
7th January, 1966, the House of Representatives approved the
Rural Land Utilization Tax Bill, presented by Mr. A. A. Hunter,

Minister of Natural Resources. From the speech that he delivered on that occasion are drawn the following paragraphs, which so vividly depict the problems and the proposed remedy.

'The early settlers on the shore of Belize saw before them great stretches of virgin forest to which they could lay claim. The mechanics of making a claim were simple. The settler staked out an area and defended it against all comers, by force of arms if necessary. With the introduction of formal government existing claims were recognized and recorded, all unoccupied land being annexed to the Crown. The rights of the small indigenous population were either ignored or overruled. Operation of these estates consisted simply of taking the bounty that nature provided. Many of these estates changed hands, but almost always the purpose of the new owners was identical with that of the old.

'Today the robber economy is dead or nearly so, but the large estates remain. Not a few of those which have come into the market have been acquired by land speculators, chiefly non-residents, looking for a quick capital gain: 11,762 acres in the Orange Walk District, bought for $49,989 in 1959, were sold in 1965 for $329,336: 14,085 acres on the Northern River went up in price from $10,000 to $200,000 in eight years. Such speculative sales would inflate the value of land, placing it out of the reach of the small man, who needs it for productive use. Expansion of the economy was being held back by selfseeking landowners, who had no interest in making use of the land for agricultural development.

'Forty per cent (3,500 square miles) of the country is privately owned in large estates, most of which were established a century or more ago. The central fact is that of 3,105,767 acres of land in agricultural holdings, only a total of 105,554 acres is cultivated, and of the total acreage in agricultural holdings, some 2,330,000 acres are in private ownership.

'The late Mr. Jack Downie, a Senior Economic Adviser in the United Kingdom Treasury, writing in 1959, gave it as his opinion that the most practical way of bringing back into circulation some of the large tracts of privately owned land, which at present lie uncultivated, was to impose heavy taxation on such land.

'The Speech from the Throne for 1962 included a passage: "The Government reiterates its strong disapproval of the land fragmentation programmes of certain land speculators and will not hesitate to pass legislation to control this aspect of land use."

'Again in 1963 the Speech from the Throne contained these words: "Government is determined to find a way to promote the development of these lands."

'The Bill before the House of Representatives is to levy a tax on undeveloped rural land for the purpose of encouraging the owners to develop the land. On land within two miles of a road the rate is $1.00 an acre for the years 1966 and 1967, $2.00 an acre for the years 1968 and 1969, and $3.00 for 1970 and later years. Land more than two miles from a highway will pay $0.50 an acre per year. The tax does not apply to holdings under 100 acres, nor to rural land on which permanent improvements have been made, or to leased national land. The exemption of land holdings of under 100 acres ensures that the vast majority of the farming populace escapes the tax. There are in fact only 365 persons holding lands exceeding 100 acres. Of these 181 are non-nationals, and 184 are nationals, but while the 184 nationals hold

Carib women. About 10,000 Caribs live in British Honduras, mostly in the Stann Creek District.

234,000 acres, the 181 non-nationals hold 2,136,000 acres. Only 50 persons hold estates of the order of 10,000 acres or larger, and together own 2,000,000 acres. Only *three* of these persons are nationals.

'The ownership of land carries with it certain social obligations. *Land is held not as a right but in trust from the community*. The trust is discharged when permanent improvements are effected to the land, so that it makes a return to the community in the form of food, of wages, of export earnings and the like. If the land cannot be sold at a price at least equal to the amount of tax owed, it reverts to the Government as the agent of the community.'

The Minister concluded his speech with these words:

'The Bill serves notice from this day on, breaking with the traditions of our past, we shall demand from those in possession of our land a contribution to the national welfare commensurate with the privilege which they enjoy. It is an act of economic emancipation marking a watershed in our history. I look forward five years from now to see its rippling effects in extensive forests under scientific management, in green fields of corn, in well established pastures carrying large herds of cattle. Let us but persevere in carrying through this measure and I am certain that in a few short years our whole future will have been transformed.'

Five years are far too few, but allowances must be made for the Minister's rhetoric, which was not out of place in the speech and certainly helped to obtain approval of the measure. The Mennonites have been labouring mightily for nine years, and have cleared only one-twelfth of their land. The first result of the Bill was to make everyone, whose holding might be liable to tax, apply for exemption. Many will obtain it. An American farmer, who had sold his 500 acres in California and with the proceeds bought 13,000 acres in Belize (such is the discrepancy in land values) and had cleared 400 acres of his holding, will obtain exemption, for he is in the process of developing the rest. A wealthy merchant of Belize, who had 1,000 acres uncultivated, which he freely owned he was holding for resale, changed his mind, and offered to stock the land with cattle, for which purpose he will have to chop down trees and sow forage. He will obtain exemption.

The most probable development will at first be cattle production, as the clearing of the forest by trashing and burning at the end of the dry season (from February to May) will allow a growth of browse in the first year, and the conversion to pasture will come with the grazing by the beasts themselves. More land will be taken by the sugar cane planters, but there will be a substantial section, held by overseas land speculators, which will either have to pay the tax or be handed over to the government, unless the owners sell off in small lots or develop it in agricultural combines.

Behind the enthusiastic speech of the Minister of Natural Resources we can see the Mennonite settlements holding up a mirror, in which we see the reflection of what can be done and has been done.

Belize needs outside capital, but it also needs people, hard working people, to build up the country. Belize still holds out one of the last opportunities for pioneering.

READING LIST

ANDERSON, A. H. *Brief Sketch of British Honduras*. Rev. ed. Belize, Printing Department, 1958.

BIANCHI, William J. *Belize: the Controversy between Guatemala and Great Britain over the Territory of British Honduras in Central America*. New York, Las Americas Publishing Co., 1959.

BLOOMFIELD, Louis M. *The British Honduras-Guatemala Dispute*. Toronto, Carswell Co. Ltd., 1953.

BURDON, Sir John A., Editor. *Archives of British Honduras*. 3 vols. London, Sifton Praed on behalf of the West India Committee, 1931–35.

CAIGER, Stephen L. *British Honduras, Past and Present*. London, Allen and Unwin, 1951.

CARR, J. D. and THORPE, John. *From the Cam to the Cays: the story of the Cambridge Expedition to British Honduras 1959–60*. London, Putnam, 1961.

CLEGERN, Wayne M. *British Honduras: Colonial Dead-end, 1859–1900*. Baton Rogue, Louisiana State University Press, 1967.

DONOHOE, W. A. *A History of British Honduras*. Montreal, Provincial Publishing Co. Ltd., 1946.

FOWLER, Henry. *A Narrative of a Journey Across the Unexplored Portion of British Honduras, with a Short Sketch of the History and Resources of the Colony*. Belize, Government Press, 1879.

GIBBS, Archibald R. *British Honduras: an Historical and Descriptive Account of the Colony from its Settlement, 1670*. London, Sampson Low, 1883.

HENDERSON, George. *An Account of the British Settlement of British Honduras . . . [with] Sketches of the Manners and Customs of the Mosquito Indians*. London, C. and R. Baldwin, 1809.

HUMPHREYS, R. A. *The Diplomatic History of British Honduras, 1638–1901*. Oxford University Press, 1961.

JONES, N. S. Carey. *The Pattern of a Dependent Economy: the National Income of British Honduras*. Cambridge University Press, 1953.

MORRIS, D. *The Colony of British Honduras: its Resources and Prospects*. London, Edward Stanford, 1883.

RODRIGUEZ, Mario. *A Palmerstonian Diplomat in Central America: Frederick Chatfield, Esq*. Tucson, University of Arizona Press, 1964.

STODDART, D. R. *Effects of Hurricane Hattie on the British Honduras Reefs and Cays, October 30–31, 1961*. Washington, National

Research Council, Pacific Science Board, 1963. (Atoll Research Bulletin no. 95.)

STODDART, D. R. *Three Caribbean Atolls: Turneffe Islands, Lighthouse Reef, and Glover's Reef, British Honduras.* Washington, National Research Council, Pacific Science Board, 1962. (Atoll Research Bulletin no. 87.)

TAYLOR, Douglas MacRae. *The Black Carib of British Honduras.* New York, Wenner-Green Foundation for Anthropological Research, 1951.

THOMPSON, J. Eric S. *The Rise and Fall of Maya Civilization.* London, Gollancz, 1956.

WADDELL, D. A. G. *British Honduras: a Historical and Contemporary Survey.* Oxford University Press, 1961.

WINZERLING, E. O. *The Beginning of British Honduras 1506–1765.* New York, North River Press, 1946.

OFFICIAL PUBLICATIONS

British Honduras. Report for the years 1964 and 1965. London, HMSO, 1968.

Development plan, 1964–1970. Belize, Office of the First Minister, 1963.

A Development Plan for British Honduras. New York, United Nations, Department of Economic and Social Affairs, 1963. 4 parts.

An Economic Policy for British Honduras, by Jack Downie. Belize, Government Printer, 1959.

Land in British Honduras. Report of the British Honduras Land Use Survey Team . . . edited by D. H. Romney. London, HMSO, 1959. 2 vols. (Colonial Research Publication no. 24.)

Report of the British Honduras Conference, 1960. London, HMSO, 1960. (Cmd. 984.)

Report of the British Honduras Constitutional Conference, 1963. London, HMSO, 1963. (Cmd. 2124.)

Report of the Tripartite Economic Survey of British Honduras. London, 1966. (Mission appointed by the governments of the UK, Canada and US.)

West India Royal Commission Report. London, HMSO, 1945. (Cmd. 6607.)

West India Royal Commission, 1938–39: Statement of Action Taken on the Recommendations. London, HMSO, 1945. (Cmd. 6656.)

INDEX

Printed in England for Her Majesty's Stationery Office
by Eyre and Spottiswoode Limited at Grosvenor Press Portsmouth
Dd. 138694. K40.
S.O. Code 88-496*